A PATHFINDER IN THE PEENEMÜNDE RAID

A PATHFINDER IN THE PEENEMÜNDE RAID

50 OPERATIONS OVER NAZI-OCCUPIED TERRITORY

ARTHUR SPENCER

Pen & Sword
MILITARY

AN IMPRINT OF PEN & SWORD BOOKS LTD.
YORKSHIRE - PHILADELPHIA

First published in Great Britain in 2024 by
PEN AND SWORD MILITARY
An imprint of
Pen & Sword Books Limited
Yorkshire – Philadelphia

Copyright © Arthur Spencer, 2024

ISBN 978 1 39907 984 6

The right of Arthur Spencer to be identified as Author of this work has been asserted by him in accordance with the Copyright, Designs and Patents Act 1988.

A CIP catalogue record for this book is available from the British Library.

All rights reserved. No part of this book may be reproduced or transmitted in any form or by any means, electronic or mechanical including photocopying, recording or by any information storage and retrieval system, without permission from the Publisher in writing.

Typeset in Times New Roman 12/16 by
SJmagic DESIGN SERVICES, India.
Printed and bound in the UK by CPI Group (UK) Ltd.

Pen & Sword Books Limited incorporates the imprints of Atlas, Archaeology, Aviation, Discovery, Family History, Fiction, History, Maritime, Military, Military Classics, Politics, Select, Transport, True Crime, Air World, Frontline Publishing, Leo Cooper, Remember When, Seaforth Publishing, The Praetorian Press, Wharncliffe Local History, Wharncliffe Transport, Wharncliffe True Crime and White Owl.

For a complete list of Pen & Sword titles please contact
PEN & SWORD BOOKS LIMITED
George House, Units 12 & 13, Beevor Street, Off Pontefract Road,
Barnsley, South Yorkshire, S71 1HN, England
E-mail: enquiries@pen-and-sword.co.uk
Website: www.pen-and-sword.co.uk

or

PEN AND SWORD BOOKS
1950 Lawrence Rd, Havertown, PA 19083, USA
E-mail: uspen-and-sword@casematepublishers.com
Website: www.penandswordbooks.com

Near the snow, near the sun, in the highest fields
See how these names are feted by the waving grass
And by the streamers of white cloud
And whispers of wind in the listening sky.
The names of those who in their lives fought for life,
Who wore at their hearts the fire's centre.
Born of the sun they travelled a short while towards the sun
And left the vivid air signed with their honour.

From 'The Truly Great' by Stephen Spender.
Reproduced with kind permission of Curtis Brown Group Ltd, London on behalf of the Beneficiaries of The Estate of Stephen Spender
Copyright © Stephen Spender, 1955.

To Jimmy Munro DFC, Ron Bennett DFM, 'Weasel' Hill DFM, with whom I flew 45 bomber operations, mainly in J-Johnnie of 97 Squadron; to F/Sgt J Underwood, with whom I flew 15; to Jimmy Silk DFM, Peter Burbridge DFC, and F/Sgt W Waller, who were shot down over Berlin on the night of 22 November 1943, and who have no known grave.

All are commemorated on the RAF Memorial at Runnymede.

Contents

Introduction		viii
Chapter 1	To begin at the beginning: 1921–1940	1
Chapter 2	The Royal Air Force: Early days 1940–1941	6
Chapter 3	The New World: June 1941–May 1942	9
Chapter 4	Training Continues: June 1942–December 1942	14
Chapter 5	Bomber Command Main Force: December 1942–April 1943	17
Chapter 6	Bomber Command Pathfinder Force: April 1943–September 1943	26
Chapter 7	Friedrichshafen-Operation Bellicose: 20 June 1943	33
Chapter 8	The Battle of Hamburg-Operation Gomorrah: August 1943	42
Chapter 9	Peenemünde-Operation Hydra: 17 August 1943	46
Chapter 10	Berlin – End of Tour: August–September 1943	53
Chapter 11	The Mediterranean Theatre Part 1: December 1943–July 1944	57
Chapter 12	Valence la Trésorie: 24 July 1944	62
Chapter 13	The Mediterranean Theatre Part 2: July 1944–December 1944	66
Chapter 14	Transport Command: January 1945–December 1945	69
Chapter 15	BOAC (British Overseas Airways Corporation): December 1945–January 1947	74
Conclusion		81
Addendum		83
Epilogue: Two different points of view		85
Bibliography		88

Introduction

My son-in law, Richard Knott, (author of *Black Night for Bomber Command*) sent me in the summer of 2001 an extract from a magazine about the Second World War Experience Centre at Leeds. Having had quite an interesting war, and never having put anything down on paper before, I contacted the Centre with a brief synopsis of my experiences.

The Director, Peter Liddle, previously a member of the History Department at Leeds University, responded immediately, and we agreed that since the Centre had no interviewer in the south-west, as it does in the south-east, I would put my recollections on audio tape. This I did, completing the work early in 2002. The Centre sent me, as arranged, a copy of the transcription made by the transcriber, Carolyn Mumford. She had done a magnificent job on the material I had provided, but as a former English teacher, I was horrified by the number of times I had said 'Well...', by the number of times I had strung a series of clauses together with 'and', and by the repetitions of which I had so frequently been guilty. I decided to re-edit the material, using Carolyn's transcription as a standing point; this also gave me the opportunity to include several more anecdotes that I had previously omitted.

Arthur Spencer,
August 2002

Chapter 1

To begin at the beginning
1921–1940

> Old men forget; yet all shall be forgot,
> But he'll remember with advantages,
> What feats he did that day.
> (King Henry V, Act 4, Scene 3,
> William Shakespeare)

I hope there won't be too many 'advantages' here, and certainly there won't be many feats; no heroics in this story; I just did as conscientiously as possible the job that the RAF trained me to do.

However, to begin, like 'Under Milk Wood', at the beginning, which is what I was asked to do. I was born in Salisbury, Wiltshire, on February 11th 1921. We - my mother, father, and I, an only son - must have moved to Southampton earlier than I can remember. Throughout my boyhood, my father was a postman there, which meant, of course, that we were never very well-off, but at least he had a regular permanent job at a time when there were three million unemployed in this country. At first he walked the rounds; later he became a van driver, which gave him a slightly better income and certainly improved his working hours; later still he became a Head Postman, an indoor supervisory role, but was compelled to retire at 60 instead of being allowed to stay till 65 because of his poor health record.

He had served in the King's Royal Rifles during the first World War. He hadn't been very fit in his early years, which probably saved him from service in the trenches in France. He spent quite a lot of his service in southern Ireland. He used to tell a rather nice story about being taken by my grandmother to Salisbury Infirmary when he was quite small; on the way home she had said to him, "Roy, I have to tell you that you will never make old bones." Well, he was 93 when he died, having received a partial disability pension from the army for 69 years, and my mother had died three months previously within a month of her 90th birthday, so they both made fairly old bones!

Before I leave my father, it might be worth recounting another story. It concerns a much earlier war, the Boer War. He had been born in 1894 and had just started school when Mafeking was relieved after its long siege. It was a small two-teacher country school at Coombe Bissett, just outside of Salisbury. On the day that Mafeking was relieved - or more likely the next day, for news travelled slowly then - the two teachers came out into the playground, one carrying a Union Jack, and the other beating a drum, and assembled the pupils - not many of them - in a ring. They announced the relief of Mafeking, sang 'God Save the Queen', and then the children were given the rest of the day as a holiday. He ran home to the next village, Dogdean, but at that early age couldn't say the word 'Mafeking' properly, so my grandmother, thinking he had run away from school, beat him and sent him back again!

My mother came from the neighbouring village of Homington and like many country girls had gone 'into domestic service' as soon as she left school. Like almost all married women in the twenties and thirties, she was a housewife who never went out to paid employment, though as the war went on she went to work in the NAAFI near Southampton Docks for two or three years. She must have been a very good manager, for she achieved quite a reasonable standard of living on what must have been a very modest income.

When I started school, I went initially to Swaythling School, about half a mile from where we lived; I was fortunate enough thoroughly to enjoy school and three of us from my year group passed what was then known as the 'Scholarship' examination, and transferred to Taunton's School, a conventional boys' grammar school. It was quite a big school for those days, eight hundred boys with a big Sixth Form. I was always keen on games and probably spent more time on the games field than I should have done, but even so managed to make fairly steady progress through school and at the age of sixteen took a reasonably successful School Certificate with Matriculation exemption. It's probably worth mentioning that the Head had said to my parents at some fairly early stage of my school career that my French wasn't too wonderful; I'm sure this was an understatement; he recommended an exchange with a French family. The school, being right on the south coast, had very good links with France, and many boys went on French exchanges every year. I was lucky enough to go for three successive years, a month each time, to the same family in the little town of La Ferté Macé in Normandy. We all got on very well with my French exchangee, and Jacques and I were in frequent touch until his death in his mid-nineties, though I must confess that our wives did most of the writing!

Some years ago my granddaughter, who then lived near York, went on a school to school exchange (these now seem more usual than the sort of individual exchange which I enjoyed) to a school near Orléans where Jacques then lived and spent a day with him and his wife. She had to compile a scrapbook about the exchange, and in it she has a photo of the two of us when we were fourteen or fifteen, and another when we were in our mid-seventies. An impressive example of life-long learning!

One incident which I recall from my earlier boyhood is a visit, on my father's motorbike, to Lee-on-Solent to watch the last of the Schneider Trophy competitions for the fastest seaplane; the last, because in 1931 the RAF won the competition outright with the Supermarine S6B, forerunner of the Spitfire, competing against Italy. It would be tempting to claim that this experience gave me a life-long passion for aviation; tempting, but quite untrue. It was an exciting and enjoyable day out, but it meant rather less to me at the time than a visit to the Dell in Southampton to watch Southampton F.C. or to the County Ground to see a county cricket match.

After Matric I went into the Sixth Form (I am horrified now to think what a sacrifice it must have been to my parents to keep me at school, but, of course, I didn't realise it then) and continued to make fairly steady progress; thanks to the exchanges, my French was vastly improved, and this was now one of my Higher School Certificate subjects. In the first year in the Sixth Form came the Munich crisis, and it was pretty clear that war was coming sooner or later. A year later, Germany invaded Poland, and war was declared. Arrangements were in hand to evacuate schools from Southampton. We were lucky enough to go only thirty miles along the coast to Bournemouth. I have a picture of some of the school walking down to Southampton Station, two or three miles from the school, quite a long distance carrying cases, and, of course, gas masks. The interesting thing about the picture is that the teacher holding the placard showing that we were Taunton's School, Southampton, is Horace King, who happened to be my sixth form English teacher, and became MP for one of the Southampton constituencies in 1950, then, during the Wilson administration, Speaker of the House of Commons, and later still, Lord Mowbray King.

Off we went to Bournemouth. We were very lucky, for our host school, Bournemouth School, had that very term moved into brand new buildings. In fact, the contractors were still working there; the paint was hardly dry. Moreover, the new school had been built on the outskirts of the town with more than adequate playing fields, something that Taunton's School had always lacked in Southampton. I heard Chamberlain's declaration of war sitting in a church hall in Bournemouth on September 3rd 1939. Eventually, after about a fortnight kicking our heels, term began. Arrangements were made for half-day schooling, alternately morning and afternoon, with Bournemouth School, which wasn't quite as bad as it sounds because the half-days were lengthened, and really we didn't miss very much schooling, especially in the Sixth Form.

A friend, Bill Blight, and I were very lucky in our accommodation. We were billeted with a very kindly landlady in her sweet shop. (Sweet rationing had already started, of course.) Bill was captain of soccer and cricket, and I was captain of hockey, so it was a very sport-orientated home. As term went on, one or two younger members of staff disappeared into the forces or into jobs with various Ministries, but on the whole school went on more or less as normal until the early part of the summer, when the Germans broke through the French lines and the evacuation from Dunkirk took place. Eight hundred French *poilus* were crammed into the building; most of them were very tired, in fact shattered; the weather was very fine, and they spent most of their time lying on the lawn outside the school sleeping. When senior boys of the school were asked to help, it gave me a very good opportunity to get quite a lot of practice in French conversation just before taking my examinations.

At about this time, news came through of the first Old Boy casualty in France, and news of another, now a Sergeant-Pilot, who had been mentioned in despatches. Later there were more casualties, one of them an Old Boy who had been a boy entrant of the Royal Navy and who had been manning a gun on a naval vessel in Portland Harbour when there was an attack by German aircraft; although badly wounded, he kept firing till he died; he was awarded the V.C. His name was Jack Mantle.

Eventually, examinations over, the school year came to an end. With about fifty or sixty other boys, I went off to a forestry camp in Cannock Chase, probably harder physical work than I had ever done before, clearing hillsides of saplings; soon after that I applied to join the RAF as aircrew. I was accepted in the pilot/navigator category, but call-up was deferred. So many young men were volunteering for aircrew service at that time that the Air Force couldn't cope with such an influx all at once.

Chapter 2

The Royal Air Force
Early days 1940–1941

I looked round for a job in the meantime and found that the Air Raid Precautions (ARP) were advertising for drivers; I was lucky enough to have a driving licence, so I was able to join the Rescue and Demolition Service for two or three months until the RAF required my services. I earned £3–3 shillings a week, which was quite a reasonable wage in 1940. While I was serving with the R & D there were several daylight raids on Southampton, and we were called into action. One was an attack on the Supermarine works at Woolston where Spitfires were made, and another was on a factory at Eastleigh Airport. However, the RAF eventually remembered my existence, and I finally joined up as an AC2/ut (under-training) pilot early in November, just a week or two before the big night raids on Southampton began.

The RAF still found us too numerous to cope with, so after a couple of false starts at Uxbridge and Blackpool, we eventually reached Wilmslow, Cheshire, for kitting out and drill, universally known as 'square-bashing'. Then we were sent off to man gun-posts at various airfields. Later the RAF Regiment undertook this task. I was sent to Watton in Norfolk, a Blenheim base, and initially to its satellite airfield, Bodney. One afternoon, the Luftwaffe raided Watton. Ken Romain, a friend of mine from the same gunpost, had gone into the parent station for a bath, there being no baths at the satellite field, and returned quite considerably shaken by his experience. One of the attacking aircraft was, in fact, brought down close to the airfield by a device known as PAC (Parachute and Cable), which comprised, as one might expect, of a strong metal cable attached to a parachute so that, when fired vertically, it descended slowly and if the timing was accurate, it ensnared an approaching aircraft; the same principle as a barrage balloon, but low level and temporary. An entrepreneurial photographic section sold postcards of the downed Heinkel 111, from which all the crew survived unhurt, at 6d. a card, and no doubt made a healthy profit! I believe that very few aircraft were downed over land using PAC, but it was markedly more successful when used for convoy protection at sea, especially when, in a later version, a small bomb was attached to the cable.

After some weeks at the satellite field, all u/t aircrew were sent back to the parent station, where life was rather less rigorous. I was lucky enough to be at the gunpost on top of the flying control tower. The regular gunners joked that we were too soft to stand the conditions at the satellite, but I think it was really so that we could be available at short notice when the inevitable posting away from Watton came.

Eventually it did come; we were at last put back on the track of aircrew training and sent off to the Aircrew Reception Centre at Babbacombe, near Torquay, really for a repetition of the drill and PE training we had already done. We felt rather old hands because some of the intake had come straight from civilian life, whereas we had all of six months service, so we put on the airs of old soldiers! After a few weeks at Babbacombe, we were sent off to ITW, Initial Training Wing, at Scarborough. We were based in the Grand Hotel, right on the cliff-top overlooking the front; we were supposed to undertake an eight-week course, but the RAF, having neglected us for so long, rushed us through in five weeks. The course included the usual subjects for pilots and navigators: navigation, airmanship, aircraft recognition, meteorology, armaments. I never fail to think of the armaments lectures when I read or hear Henry Reed's poem, "Naming of Parts". In the third verse there is a minor grammatical error, exactly like the corporal who taught us about weapons would make.

Rumour had it that we would be going to the USA to do our aircrew training, and this proved to be so; we were, in fact, only the second group to go under the Arnold Scheme - so-called after General "Hap" Arnold, the commander of the United States Army Air Corps from 1938 till 1945, who had himself been taught to fly by the Wright Brothers in 1911. America was not yet at war, so we could not go in uniform, and were all kitted out in grey flannel suits, all exactly the same colour and pattern, so really a uniform in itself! We were also, because the British military establishment knew all about service in the tropics, and much to the amusement of the inhabitants of Florida when we eventually got there, issued with pith-helmets; what became of them I can't recall.

Chapter 3

The New World
June 1941–May 1942

We sailed from Gourock, Scotland, in a tiny vessel which used to ply between Liverpool and Belfast, and went to Iceland where we were accommodated in a transit camp some 15 miles outside of Reykjavik. It was a fairly horrendous journey; the sea was very rough indeed and nearly everyone was seasick. There was an Anson flying round and round the convoy; I couldn't help wondering just how effective it would be if we really were attacked. Fortunately, there were no problems. When we reached Iceland, we were told immediately that Reykjavik was out of bounds, since it was thought to be, like Lisbon, a hot-bed of espionage. The majority of us were quite content to be off the sea, and very content to be close to hot springs where we could wash, shave, and have an occasional swim.

It was May, so we saw very little darkness; after only a couple of days we were on our way again, bound for Halifax, Nova Scotia. This time we were much luckier in our transport. Only about a hundred of us were put on board an armed merchant cruiser, the Ranpura, sistership of the Rawalpindi which had been sunk earlier during the war. Our ship was armed with one very large gun amidships and we sailed in the middle of the convoy. The Ranpura was large enough to be quite comfortable; just after we had embarked, the ship's commander called us all together, and said something like; "Gentleman, I must apologise, I realise you are all potential officers, but I haven't possibly got room for you all in the wardroom, but we shall make you as comfortable as possible." We were highly amused, for we weren't used to such treatment in the Air Force. It seemed that the Navy was going to treat us in a much more gentlemanly way!

There was one moment of excitement on the way across to Halifax. A couple of days out the sirens sounded, and we all assembled at our boat stations. However, it wasn't a real crisis; the very large American convoy on its way to take over Iceland had come into view, and we were soon released back to whatever we did to occupy our spare time. Arriving at Halifax, we were put on a train for a couple of days to go to Toronto. When we reached that attractive city, we were sent to a huge RCAF reception centre in the buildings of an old exhibition site, known as Manning Pool. As we marched in probably a bit sloppily, tired after our long journey, a voice shouted, "You just over, lads?" We nodded agreement, and a terrific burst of spontaneous applause broke out all round the arena from these hundreds of new Canadian recruits. I'm sure we marched with an extra touch of pride in our steps after that.

A few days later, but not before a friend and I had managed to hitchhike to Niagara Falls one evening, we were off on the train again, but this time in a southerly direction, to Lakeland School of Aeronautics in Florida. Here we were under the supervision of the United States Army Air Corps, and followed exactly the same course that the American cadets undertook. One week we flew in the mornings - very early, before the Florida sun caused too much turbulence - and studied the same sort of subjects we had studied at ITW in the afternoon; the next week, ground school was in the morning, and flying, under the instruction of very experienced civilian instructors, took place in the afternoon. At this stage, I coped as well as most with the Stearman 17s which we flew, and soloed with no problems. After ten weeks, the four of us assigned to Bill Lethio all 'graduated' and went on to Basic Training.

The local people in the little town of Lakeland were exceptionally hospitable, and most weekends we were invited to stay in American homes where comforts were lavished upon us. I was particularly fortunate, being the only member of the course from Southampton; it so happened that immediately adjacent to our quarters was an orange grove where the wife of the owner was from my hometown. It was very rare not to find a pile of oranges and grapefruit on my bunk at some time during the day, and I had many memorable meals with them in their bungalow.

At the end of the course, we were given a long weekend's leave, so a friend and I hitch-hiked to Miami - we were by no means the only ones - where we spent two happy days, mainly on the beach, after we had found a hotel owned by a Mancunian who was willing to accommodate us at a very preferential rate.

The next stage of training took us to Montgomery, Alabama to fly Vultee B.T.13s, monoplanes, which I found much more difficult to handle, and had a much less sympathetic instructor, a young American second-lieutenant, who had only just finished pilot training himself. I soloed successfully and got about half way through the course before it was decided that my flying skills were not up to the required standard; I was eliminated, and sent back to Canada for remustering.

There were half a dozen of us on the train journey back to Ontario, one of whom was a young man already beginning to carve out a career for himself on the stage, Michael Aldridge; I saw him once or twice after the war when he was performing at Bristol Theatre Royal; he never quite became a star, but late in his career he did achieve some fame as the garrulous retired headmaster in the BBC series "Last of the Summer Wine". As a navigator he had flown in the Balkan Air Force stationed in the heel of Italy, dropping supplies to partisans in Albania, Greece and Yugoslavia and sometimes even further afield.

Remustering took place at Trenton, Ontario; we were there in December 1941, and were given 5 days leave over Christmas. A friend and I decided that this would be the chance of a lifetime to see New York, so we set off to hitch-hike there. Recrossing the border back into the USA took a little time, but eventually we got on our way. There was no shortage of lifts; almost every American who picked us up wanted us to go and spend Christmas with them; they were extraordinarily generous in their desire to be hospitable. (This was only weeks after Pearl Harbour, of course.) However, we insisted that we wanted to get to New York, and once there had three very exciting days. The United Services Organisation provided ample hospitality - free tickets to shows on Broadway, free meals, free tours. Our three days sped by, and all too soon we had to set off back to Canada, hitch-hiking once more through the Appalachians, and so to Trenton.

Soon I was on my way back to Florida again, this time to the United States Naval Air Service training school at Pensacola, where I did successfully complete the course as a navigator. One of my friends at Pensacola was George Brantingham; we stayed at the same units till he completed a tour of operations, and were in close touch until his death in 2013, he and his wife having retired to a Somerset village less than thirty miles from our own home. The course was very, very strong on theory, and we spent a great deal of time on astro-navigation, but much less strong on practice. My logbook shows less than 30 hours flying at Pensacola, most of that over the sea, and no night-flying, whereas if I had been at an RAF or RCAF school, I would have had between 120 and 150 hours training in the air. In spite of this, the RAF deemed half a dozen of us capable of navigating aircraft which were being ferried back to the UK. We were sent to RAF Ferry Command Headquarters at Dorval, near Montreal. There I crewed up with a very experienced civilian pilot, an equally experienced civilian wireless operator, and a second pilot who, like me, had just finished his training. We were allocated a Ventura to deliver to the UK. We did no training flights but were briefed several times, learnt to use the oxygen system and did some dinghy drill, then, after a fortnight, we set out in this little two-engined Lockheed, rather like a Hudson, to fly to Gander, Newfoundland. The range of the aircraft was so limited that everyone flew to Gander to shorten the Atlantic crossing, and even from there, a tail-wind component was needed! Quite a few of the pilots went via Iceland, or even via Bluey West, the American base in Greenland, but my pilot decided he wanted to fly straight across. We waited a fortnight for a favourable wind. In spite of the limitations of my training, we managed to make a landfall in Northern Ireland, and so on to Prestwick. Waiting at Gander at the same time was my friend George Brantingham, and it was that fortnight there that cemented our friendship. There must have been just the two crews there waiting to cross, so we followed the same routine; visit the Met Office; draw up a flight plan; our pilots would make a decision about the feasibility of crossing; go for a walk round the lake; try again the next day! Eventually George's pilot tired of waiting and decided to cross via Iceland, but my skipper was anxious to get right across in one hop. Nevertheless, we did not have to wait long once George had gone. All aircrew arriving back in the UK from wherever they were trained were sent to Bournemouth, which, of course, was no hardship to me because I was able to spend a night or two at home in Southampton, and to visit my old school, still evacuated to Bournemouth. One incident which occurred during my brief stay there I do recall quite vividly; one afternoon, two Messerschmitt 109s swept in from the sea low over the roof-tops, each carrying a single bomb, which they deposited on hotels where air crew just arrived were billeted. They succeeded in killing a few young Canadians, newly arrived, who hadn't yet got into the war at all.

Chapter 4

Training Continues
June 1942–December 1942

From Bournemouth we were sent on to Advanced Flying Units, in my case to Bobington, later called Halfpenny Green, near Stourbridge, in the Midlands. These units were intended to familiarise aircrew who had trained in the good weather of Florida, South Africa, Rhodesia and elsewhere, where there were no nightly black-outs, with the very different conditions in this country. Once again, however, the course was considerably shortened; eight weeks again became five and then Bomber Command demanded our presence. All the members of our course were posted as sergeants since there was no time for commissioning interviews. I rather resented this at the time, but in the end it worked out much to my advantage, for had I been a pilot-officer I might well not have crewed up with the outstanding young Canadian who became my pilot, then a sergeant like myself.

The next stage of training was OTU, Operational Training Unit, at Upper Heyford, a few miles outside of Oxford. This was very much a pilot-orientated course, and quite rightly so, because the pilots, who previously had not flown anything bigger than an Oxford, had to convert to a much bigger, heavier, operational aircraft, the Wellington. It was also important for the opportunity to crew up. Wellington crews at that time had five members: pilot, navigator, bomb-aimer, wireless operator, and rear-gunner. George said to me one day very soon after we had arrived at OTU, "I have got myself a pilot." He had teamed up with a larger-than-life American who had gone north of the border to join the RCAF. I approached this American at the next opportunity and said that I had heard he had got a navigator; could he recommend a pilot to me? He thought for a moment and said, "Well, I reckon young Jimmy Munro is one of the best pilots on our course." That brief conversation is probably the reason I'm still here today! I saw Jimmy as soon as possible. No, he hadn't a navigator at that stage, and would be happy to take me on. I was keen to get a bomb-aimer who had also done navigation training; there were a lot of excess navigators finishing training at that time and some of them were converted to bomb-aimers. It seemed to me that we might as well have a second navigator rather than someone who had done only bomb-aimer training. Jimmy said at once, "Well, you find someone." In fact I already had my eye on a bomb-aimer wearing an Observer's brevet, which indicated that he was a qualified navigator, Eric Suswain, so that made three in the crew. In the meantime, Jimmy had spotted a likely wireless operator, Snowy (I'm not sure that I ever knew his real Christian name) Nevard, son of an Ipswich publican, whose chief interest in life was horse-racing, and a rear gunner. The latter was a wizened little figure, Wesley Hill; I well remember my first conversation with him; he said, "Everyone calls me Weasel!" He had been brought up in the Rockies with a gun in his hand, and to see him at clay-pigeon shooting was a revelation; he never missed one whereas if I hit one in twenty shots I was doing pretty well!

Once the pilots were converted to Wellingtons, we flew a number of cross-country flights together, some of them at night. Occasionally these night exercises were known as 'bullseyes.' These took aircraft over what would normally be highly defended areas; the searchlights attempted to cone the aircraft, and no doubt the anti-aircraft gunners honed their radar skills, but they didn't, of course, actually open fire. I've often wondered if the local citizens, seeing all the searchlight activity, but hearing no ac-ac asked themselves what was going on. Towards the end of the course all crews did what was known as a 'nickel', a leaflet operation over France or some other occupied territory. In our case we went to Nantes, and since we had to fly between that city and the highly defended port of St. Nazaire, a German U-boat base, so that the leaflets were blown downwind, we were subject to quite a lot of flak; we even heard several bursts in the Wellington, so they must have been fairly close to us, but we got home without any damage.

Our social life at Upper Heyford centred almost entirely on Oxford, there being transport to the city every evening, and a return bus quite late. George and I decided that as non-dancers we were 'socially constipated' and determined to put this right, so, most evenings, when we weren't flying, we attended Brett's Dancing Academy, and by the time we left Upper Heyford, we were probably better dancers than navigators.

Towards the end of our course at OTU we were on the airfield one afternoon when almost one hundred Lancasters swept across at low level and in loose formation. They were on their way to a low-level daylight attack on Le Creusot, and the impressive sight, the first time we had seen Lancasters en masse, more than confirmed our hope that we would be bound for a Lancaster squadron, rather than one equipped with Halifaxes or Stirlings.

We were lucky; at the end of our sixteen-week course we were posted to a Heavy Conversion Unit at Swinderby, just outside of Lincoln, a Lancaster HCU. This course, like OTU, was strongly pilot-orientated, for the pilot now had to take a further step forward, and learn to fly a larger four-engined aircraft. Jimmy took to Lancasters like a duck to water. We flew circuits round the airfield, both by day and by night; we did several bombing practices over the Wash, but didn't undertake any longer cross-country flights. While there we picked up two more crew, Ron Bennett, a mid-upper gunner, and Harry Townsley, a flight engineer. Just before Christmas 1942, three crews from that course made the short railway journey from Lincoln to Woodhall Spa, where we joined 97 Squadron. One of the crews was that of Bill Tracey, the American I mentioned, with my friend George Brantingham as his navigator; the third was Doug Jones. The real war was getting nearer.

Chapter 5

Bomber Command Main Force
December 1942–April 1943

So here we were at last on an operational squadron. 97 Squadron was one of the first in Bomber Command to be equipped with Lancasters and had been one of the two squadrons to take part in the famous daylight raid on Augsburg in April 1942; some of the crews who had taken part in that operation were still with the Squadron, including the Squadron Navigation Officer, Flight Lieutenant Paul Cutting, DFC. The other squadron, 44, from Waddington, lost five of their six aircraft; their CO, the sole survivor from 44, flew a badly damaged aircraft home, and was awarded the VC. 97 lost only one of their six, Squadron Leader Sherwood, a flight commander, whose aircraft was blown up over the target. He was the only survivor from his crew, and was awarded the DSO.

Now one might have thought that 97 Squadron would be keen to unleash us against the enemy as soon as possible; not so! They were not going to let a new crew, a 'sprog' crew to use the current slang, loose on one of their precious Lancasters without checking them out pretty thoroughly. We did a couple more cross-country flights, and three more 'bullseyes' - one over Portsmouth and Birmingham, another over the Humber Estuary, and the third over Plymouth and Southampton - before they decided we were fit to go. As was usual for new crews at that time, we went 'gardening'. That is, our first operation was mine-laying. I suppose that we were lucky that we didn't go to one of the north German estuaries or to the Baltic; those trips could be quite 'dicey'. We went to the much quieter Gironde estuary and placed four 1500 lb mines across the mouth of the river. We were short of petrol on the way back, and landed at Beaulieu in the New Forest, a Coastal Command station. The ground crew there had never seen a Lancaster before, and swarmed all over it, making it unserviceable! We had to wait several days till our own ground crew came down from Lincolnshire; it meant that once more I was able to spend a couple of nights at home in Southampton. In the meantime, the other two crews who had joined 97 Squadron with us had been fully blooded with a raid on Berlin.

Eventually, after a week's leave, our first real operation over Germany came at the end of January. It was, like so many subsequent trips, to the Ruhr; to Düsseldorf. We carried one 4,000 lb bomb, and 12 small bomb containers (sbc) each of 90 four-pound incendiary bombs. As we were approaching the target, and having given Jimmy the course out of the target area, there was no more I could do till the bombs were released, so I handed over to the bomb-aimer and asked Jimmy if I could move up to the front to have a look; normally, of course, I was working over charts and maps so I was behind a black-out curtain. He agreed, and I moved forward to be absolutely horrified; there seemed to be searchlights and flak all over the sky, and I just couldn't comprehend how an aircraft could survive in such a maelstrom of fire. When I thought about it more calmly afterwards, I realised that much of what one could see was really puffs of smoke from shells which had burst long before we entered the target area, and that it wasn't quite as bad as it appeared to a novice navigator at first glance. Eventually, I even got used to it! Bombs gone, we were much lighter, and with nose slightly down we sped home; I see from my log-book that the flight lasted 4 hours 55 minutes.

The attack on Düsseldorf, in which six four-engined bombers of the 162 participating were lost, was the first occasion when Pathfinders using the new device, Oboe, marked the target for the main force with Target Indicators exploding at about 3000 feet above the target.

It was a successful concentrated raid, the first of many that spring and early summer. We were right in at the beginning of the Battle of the Ruhr.

New crews at a squadron normally flew any aircraft that was available before graduating to 'their own' machine; we flew two or three raids in this way, but soon found an aircraft we liked, so Jimmy approached the Flight Commander to enquire if we might be allocated J-Johnnie; he was quite willing to do this and thereafter J-Johnnie, and, of course, its associated ground crew, was our regular Lancaster.

Three nights after the attack on Düsseldorf, we went further afield to Hamburg and returned with several small flak holes in the fuselage, but luckier than the five Lancasters which failed to return. This was another first; the first time that Pathfinders used the blind map-reading device, H2S. At the beginning of February we returned to the Ruhr, to Cologne, making the homeward flight on three engines, not because of any enemy action, but on account of an engine failure. The very next night we should have operated against Hamburg again, but the starboard inner engine developed high oil pressure, so we were forced to drop our bombs in the North Sea and make for home.

In the middle of the month, over 450 aircraft, of which seven were lost, attacked the German submarine base at Lorient and the very next night we made our first crossing of the Alps to attack the great Italian city of Milan in the Plain of Lombardy. On February 18th, we were back to the coast of the North Sea, this time to Wilhelmshaven, and a few nights later made the long journey - over seven hours - to Nuremberg. A week later we returned to Cologne and, as on the previous occasion, made the homeward flight with only three engines functioning.

The end of the month saw us back to one of the German submarine bases on the Atlantic coast of France, St Nazaire. We had, of course, experienced the accuracy of the defences there when we had undertaken our leaflet raid in a Wellington from Operational Training Unit (OTU). This time the gunners were even more accurate and left a gaping hole in the port inner engine nacelle. It was certainly very impressive when we inspected it at dispersal after landing back at Woodhall, but surprisingly had not affected the performance of the engine on the flight home. It just goes to show how tough the Lancaster was!

At the beginning of March, we paid our first visit to the Big City, to Berlin, one of over 300 aircraft on this operation, of which 19 were lost. This was the most successful attack on Berlin to date - the result of Pathfinders being equipped with H2S and the much greater weight of bombs now being carried; considerable damage was done to the railway repair workshops at Tempelhof, while twenty other factories were badly damaged. Two nights later, we went back to Hamburg - at least we thought we had bombed Hamburg, for that was the target given at briefing. However, the Pathfinders mistakenly marked Wedel, a small town several miles downstream from the target; in spite of this error, some damage was done; a large naval clothing store was completely burnt out, and a number of industrial workshops were destroyed near Wedel harbour.

Our next operation was certainly the most important we took part in that spring; it was the raid on Essen on the night of 5th/6th March. Essen was, of course, the home of Germany's greatest armaments manufacturer, Krupps. Until that night only a handful of small bombs had hit Essen, doing virtually no damage whatsoever. Tonight was different. The 'Oboe' Mosquitoes marked Krupps accurately and on time; the 'backers-up' - four-engined aircraft - placed their markers exactly on those dropped by 'Oboe' and almost 450 bombers maintained a concentrated attack over 40 minutes. Although 14 aircraft were lost, this was an acceptable price for such a devastating operation. We were lucky enough to get an aiming-point picture, which earned us a certificate from 5 Group Headquarters, standard practice in the Group at that time.

Three nights later we had another abortive sortie; we set off for Nuremberg, but had not gone far when one of the engines developed an internal coolant leak, forcing us into an early return. The next night was more successful; another long flight, just over 7 hours, took us to Munich. Much damage was done to the old city, including the BMW aero-engine factory, the HQ of the Flak brigade, and over 140 small back-street workshops for the loss of eight aircraft. This was our fifteenth trip; we were half way through our tour!

During this period, the normal routine would be to report to the Flight offices at about 9.30 am and, if operations were scheduled, fly an airtest during the morning, when all the aircraft's equipment was checked out by the specialist members of the crew. The two gunners would swivel their turrets and check their guns; the Wireless Operator would receive and despatch a message by his Marconi radio; I would check my airspeed indicator, altimeter, compasses and radar, the bomb aimer his bomb-sight and the front turret, and, most importantly, Jimmy would check all his controls to make sure that J-Johnnie was fully airworthy. Soon after a fairly quick lunch, we would be in the briefing room to learn the target and the details of the operation. An 'operational meal' followed shortly after; we made our way back to the airfield to don flying kit, collect equipment, and await a truck to take us out to the aircraft parked at its dispersal point. We would soon be on our way and would climb in the vicinity of the airfield to about 20,000 feet; in a fully laden Lancaster this would take about an hour; then we would set course. The purpose of this was to conceal as long as possible the direction of our approach; we would be travelling faster if we were flying level than if we were climbing in the same direction. The theory was that the enemy would then have less time to prepare for our reception. In fact they always seemed pretty well prepared to me; it was just as well that they did not have longer!

It was almost a fortnight - we did have a week's leave - after the Munich operation before we took part in another attack on Germany.

A PATHFINDER IN THE PEENEMÜNDE RAID

The Battle of the Ruhr continued with a short trip to Duisburg; flak did quite a lot of damage to the perspex at the front of the Lancaster and we had a rather draughty journey home. Two nights later we made the long trip to Berlin again in atrocious weather conditions; 21 aircraft were lost, some of them, no doubt, on account of the weather.

The beginning of April saw us over Essen again, the first time that Bomber Command were able to muster over 200 Lancasters in a force of nearly 350, of whom 21 did not return. This was the only occasion when we carried anything larger than a standard 4000lb 'cookie'. We transferred to a specially adapted aircraft and took an 8000 lb bomb to the target.

In the same week, we attacked Kiel; nearly 600 aircraft took part, the largest number since the artificially inflated 1000-bomber raids of 1942 - and over 400 of these were four-engined. However the weather was not helpful to an accurate attack, and the operation was not considered a success. Our twentieth operation took us back to Duisburg, and coincidentally the flak gunners there managed once again to damage some of the forward perspex without doing us serious harm; we could tolerate a bit of broken glass. Two nights later, we were over Frankfurt, but our photos showed nothing but unbroken cloud.

Our final operation in Main Force was another long trip over the Alps to the Italian naval port of La Spezia, where, with a smoke screen blowing across the target, Sus insisted on making six runs to try to get it right; we suffered quite a lot of minor flak damage, and landed at Tangmere on return short of petrol, no doubt because of those six runs! This was our last operation from Woodhall Spa and indeed in the Main Force of Bomber Command. We had survived 22 operations, and had, I think, been a reasonably successful crew; we had been coned by searchlights two or three times, which was a fairly terrifying experience, and had occasionally suffered minor flak damage, but nothing of too serious a nature.

During that period of three months, 97 Squadron had lost six aircraft. One of these was Sergeant Plaunt, a Canadian, in the raid on Essen on March 12th; he lived, like most of the NCOs, in a Nissen hut set in a little copse just off the road from Coningsby to Woodhall; at the end of the lane leading to the huts was a searchlight site. There were three such sites around the airfield, primarily for airfield defence, but also to form a cone over the airfield when we were returning from operations. Sergeant Plaunt had befriended and been befriended by the searchlight crew, and I remember how upset these soldiers were when they heard he had gone missing.

The last loss the Squadron suffered before we moved from Woodhall was Flying Officer Norton, who was lost after a raid on Berlin on March 29th. We returned from Berlin immediately behind him and were told to circle at a certain height while Flying Control dealt with his aircraft. He called up for permission to land, and was given permission, but did not acknowledge; Flying Control called him again, and yet again, but still there was silence. Since we were next in the queue in our J-Johnnie we were now given clearance to land. We found later that Norton's aircraft had crashed in the village with the loss of the whole crew. Why he crashed I never knew. He was quite an experienced pilot. Perhaps he had a bomb hanging up on board which exploded; perhaps it was a momentary loss of concentration; perhaps the delayed result of some flak damage over the target; I have often wondered; he had been to Berlin and back successfully, and was lost at the last moment on his way home.

One of the advantages of life as aircrew was, of course, that when you were not 'dicing' (i.e. dicing with death) you led a very civilised life; nothing was too good for operational aircrew and you were not under constant fire like the troops in the trenches during the first World War. Our own social activity was based mainly upon the Sergeants' Mess and a local pub, the Leagate, in Coningsby. The Mess was very friendly, largely because it was small; we were a two-flight squadron, that is one made up of about sixteen or seventeen crews, and would be expected to send out eleven or twelve aircraft on a raid requiring maximum effort. While the officers messed at the requisitioned Petwood Hotel at Woodhall Spa, our mess was closer to Coningsby with the airfield in between. Most of the nights when we were not flying we would go to the Leagate. I went there again for the first time since April 1943 in September 2001; from the outside the inn was instantly recognisable and the bar, too, had not changed. Elsewhere there were great changes; it was now a hotel with bedrooms, and the area where we used to eat off rough tables was now a smart restaurant.

The landlord at the Leagate used to be able to provide us with a very substantial mixed grill during those first few months of 1943; he told me that on one occasion he had been visited by a Ministry of Food Inspector who had asked who most of his customers were. The landlord explained that they were mainly sergeants from the local airfield who patronised the pub on nights when they were not flying; the Inspector immediately increased his ration allowance, which I thought was a very generous gesture indeed.

Occasionally I would ride my bike to the Leagate, and on one such occasion it was stolen. There were a lot of Irish navvies working on airfield construction in Lincolnshire, and when I reported the loss to the police, they said "Oh, I expect we shall find it in one of the Irish camps," and so they did and returned it to me. Later I lost it for good when it was taken from outside the briefing room while we were being briefed to go to Berlin. I felt this was adding insult to injury by stealing my bike at this time! It wasn't as if it was a service bicycle; it was my own bike on which I had cycled to school for many years. Once I had settled on an airfield, my parents sent it to me by train from Southampton. It arrived safely at Woodhall Spa Station, so I hitch-hiked from Coningsby to collect it.

The nearest town to the airfield was Boston and a 'liberty' bus ran there every evening. We used it once or twice to go to Boston to visit the cinema. I usually went with 'Sus', our bomb-aimer, but I can't remember a single film I saw there, and the occasions were pretty rare.

During March three crews, captained by Flight Lieutenants Maltby, newly arrived at the squadron, McCarthy, and Munro, began intensive low-level training. They were not screened from operations but went off most days when there were no ops to practise at almost zero feet. On one of these flights, the navigator of one of the crews, by coincidence another Munro, but a New Zealander, was injured in what nowadays we would call a bird-strike. His crew were scheduled to go on operations, and I was detailed to go with him since we were not operating that night. We flew an air-test in the morning, but operations were cancelled ('scrubbed' was the term we used then) even before we got to briefing, so the name of one of the Dambusters appears in my log-book, but only for an air-test. For that is what these three crews were practising for, we later realised.

Eventually they went off to Scampton to join 617 Squadron under the command of Guy Gibson. McCarthy and Maltby both successfully completed the dams raid and both were decorated with the DSO; the latter, however, was killed in September when his aircraft plunged into the sea; Munro was unlucky enough to be hit by light flak crossing the Dutch coast which destroyed his intercom, so he had no alternative but to return to Scampton, though he went on to have a very distinguished career as a Flight Commander in 617 under both Gibson and Leonard Cheshire. Another successfully to complete the dams raid was Dudley Heal who had been on the navigation course with me at Pensacola; his pilot was Flight Sergeant Brown, a Canadian who won the Conspicuous Gallantry Medal for his part in the operation.

Chapter 6

Bomber Command Pathfinder Force
April 1943–September 1943

At the beginning of April, rumours began to circulate that 97 Squadron would soon be on the move; in the middle of the month, Air Marshal Cochrane, the Air Officer Commanding 5 Group, came to Woodhall and announced to the assembled squadron that we would be joining Pathfinder Force (PFF) in the near future; in fact by no means the whole squadron made the move; three crews were just off to 617; three crews were so close to the end of their tour that it was decided they should not join Pathfinders, but stay at Woodhall to form the nucleus of the new squadron (619) there and finish their tours with them, while one or two crews that we had lost recently had not yet been replaced. It was, therefore, by no means a complete squadron that flew off to Bourn, a satellite of Oakington, just outside of Cambridge, on April 18th. As a WAAF in Flying Control at Woodhall who had befriended me subsequently wrote, "The last I saw of you was disappearing in a fairly ropy formation towards the south." She was quite right; it was a fairly ropy formation, but after all, night bomber pilots were, unlike their American daylight counterparts, not particularly skilled at formation flying, even though it had been stressed before we left that we ought to put on a good show for our departure.

We landed at Bourn, 5 miles west of Cambridge, then on the A45, the main road towards St. Neots and Bedford and soon found that 97 was to be transformed from the small two-flight squadron it had been all the time we were at Woodhall to a much larger three-flight unit, so that we now had between 27 and 30 aircraft on strength, and would be expected to send out about 18 or 20 aircraft on operations requiring maximum effort.

We were placed in the new 'C' Flight, which was notable because it was commanded by a navigator, Wing Commander Alabaster, DFC, previously the Group Navigation Officer. Most of the new crews that had joined the squadron at this time were returning for a second or even third tour of operations. Some of them had flown with 97 before; one such was Flight Lieutenant Rodley who had been one of the pilots to take part in the Augsburg raid a year before. The inevitable consequence of the enlargement of the Squadron was that the messes were much bigger, and some of the crew didn't take very kindly to the new Sergeants' Mess which was certainly rather a barn of a place compared with the warm, cosy mess we had left at Woodhall. The Officers must have been even more dismayed to have left the comforts of a top-class country hotel for a ramshackle wooden wartime building with fairly primitive billets around it.

Crews joining Pathfinder Force normally went to RAF Upwood, the Pathfinder Training School, but because we had moved as a squadron, the staff of the school visited us. Wing Commander Mahaddie came as 'Headmaster', a very much decorated officer, and we saw a great deal of Air Vice Marshal Bennett, the Air Officer Commanding 8 Group. I was very surprised how frank they were in talking to us, even in front of us Sergeants; they were both very critical of those regular officers who commanded their stations and who were more interested in discipline and the smartness of their stations rather than the operational efficiency of the squadrons based there. Most of these Group Captains who commanded the stations had no experience of operational flying during World War II whereas Mahaddie, an ex-Halton 'brat', had an extremely impressive row of decorations, and Bennett had been awarded a DSO when he was shot down over Norway and walked home. Whereas at both Operational Training Unit and at Heavy Conversion Unit, the emphasis had been on the pilots, and quite rightly so, since they were learning to fly a much larger operational aircraft, now the importance of navigators and bomb-aimers was stressed; pilots, said Bennett, were merely chauffeurs to get the really important people, the navigators and bomb-aimers, there to put the target-indicators (TIs), flares and bombs down in the right place; all very encouraging for the morale of those of us who were in these two 'trades', as the Air Force called them!

We spent a fortnight in very intensive training both on the ground and in the air. We flew several cross-country exercises, some of them very long distance, and we learnt to use new equipment: the Mark 14A bombsight, the air position indicator, new radar devices. The emphasis was very much on navigational accuracy, and much higher standards were expected than had been the case in the main force or at OTU. We were expected to work to the nearest 1/10 of a minute rather than 1/2, and to the nearest ½ nautical mile, for we now worked in knots and nautical miles rather than imperial measure. All members of the crew were expected to contribute to accurate navigation, and 'Weasel' would often call me up with a drift measurement, which he was able to obtain by sighting his guns on some object which we had passed directly over and measuring the drift from a calibration on his turret. I recall that on one of the cross countries, we were 70 miles off the east coast of Scotland at 20,000 feet on a brilliantly fine day, and we could see right across to the west coast and beyond; a marvellous sight.

After a fortnight, on May 5th, we did our first operation from Bourn, to Dortmund, the first raid on which more than 2,000 tons of bombs were dropped in a single operation. We didn't, on this first operation with PFF, carry any TIs, just a very heavy load of HE bombs, 1x 4000lb, 4x1000lb, 6x500lb, and 2x250lb. Nearly 600 aircraft - over 250 Lancasters - took part in this first attack on Dortmund, 31 being lost. That night is particularly memorable because we had our first and only serious encounter with a German night-fighter. We had just left the target - it was a good job that enormous load of bombs had gone! - when there was a shout from the rear gunner, 'Turn to port and dive!' Jimmy didn't need telling twice; we were almost over on our backs and screaming away to the left; both our gunners were firing, and the aircraft filled with the smell of cordite. Within moments it was all over; the German fighter disappeared into the darkness and didn't come back for a second attempt. It wasn't, I thought, a good omen for our career in Pathfinder Force.

The interesting thing from my point of view was that at that moment, when everything was happening, I didn't feel particularly afraid. There had been many previous occasions when we were making our way across Germany when one of the gunners had called up to say, "There's an aircraft out on the port (starboard) side, Jimmy; I can't see what it is but I'll keep an eye on it." On many such occasions, I had felt very afraid, but now that it was all happening, I didn't; I suppose it all happened so quickly, and there was such a rush of adrenaline that I didn't have time to be scared! There was one occasion when both gunners were certain that there was a German fighter flying along almost parallel with us, but presumably it didn't see us, nor spot us on its radar, or, more likely, was already following some other aircraft. Anyway, it didn't bother us, so, I'm sure wisely, we didn't bother it.

We had a week's leave after the Dortmund raid and returned to go to the same city towards the end of the month. (Meanwhile 617 Squadron had attacked the Ruhr dams, so we now knew what all that low-level practice had been about.) In fact, for the next couple of months, with the short nights of summer, my log-book looks like a Baedecker Guide to the Ruhr. This time we did carry TIs, so we began to feel like real Pathfinders. This second raid on Dortmund involved even more than the first; 826 bombers took part, the largest number to be used during the Battle of the Ruhr. Inevitably losses were higher, and 38 aircraft failed to return. The clear weather enabled the force to attack very accurately, and vast areas of Dortmund were destroyed, including a major steel works.

Two nights later we returned to the first target we had attacked in the Ruhr, Düsseldorf, but whereas in January we had been one of 160, now we were one of 760, including more than 300 Lancasters. Another large force participated in the raid on Wuppertal four nights later which cost 33 bombers. This operation was one of the highlights of the Battle of the Ruhr; for the first time a 'fire-storm' developed, and destroyed five of the six largest factories in the town, as well as over 200 other industrial premises.

Early in June, we returned yet again to Düsseldorf; nearly 800 aircraft took part, and losses again reached nearly 40. This was another successful raid with 40 square kilometres of the town on fire. Forty-two war industries suffered complete stoppages and thirty-five more partial reduction, while twenty military establishments were hit, eight ships sunk, and the local government headquarters destroyed. The next night we were part of a smaller force - but still more than 500 aircraft, all except the Oboe Mosquitoes four-engined - which attacked Bochum. This was yet another success in spite of cloud over the target, photo-reconnaissance showing 130 acres of the town destroyed.

In the middle of May, Jimmy's commission had come through, Pilot Officer James Francis Munro RCAF; it wasn't long before I too was commissioned, appropriately dated April 1st. My friend George Brantingham was commissioned the same day; he lived near me in Somerset and used to pull my leg that he was senior to me because although we were commissioned on the same day, his number was 145358, whereas mine is 145359. I reply that it's only because 'B' comes before 'S' in the alphabet.

We returned from one of our operations to the Ruhr to find East Anglia fogbound and were diverted to RAF High Ercall in Shropshire. I was very impressed that the station was able to cope with fifty or sixty Lancasters arriving probably at very short notice, debriefing us, giving us all an operational breakfast of eggs and bacon, accommodating us, and even providing us with some basic toilet kit so that we could have a shave and wash and brush-up before returning to Cambridgeshire the next afternoon.

Operations went on, but intensive training also continued. We flew more bullseyes over Plymouth, Liverpool and Manchester. These flights usually included a 'bombing' run on Goole Docks! A camera would show how accurate this was by picking up an infra-red light on the target; we must have 'bombed' Goole dozens of times! Another form of training was fighter affiliation. We would climb laboriously up to approximate operational altitude and then notify base that we were there; a Spitfire or Hurricane would then take off from a nearby fighter station and attempt to shoot one down, not literally, of course, but it carried a camera gun, and a subsequent analysis of the film would reveal how successful he had been, and also how successful the bomber had been in evading his attentions.

It was normal on these occasions as a measure of economy to carry two rear gunners; one would be at the guns in the turret, while the other waited his turn just outside. Jimmy was something of a fighter pilot manqué and would throw the Lancaster around the sky as if it were a fighter. On one such occasion, the rear gunner of another crew was installed in the turret, while Weasel, our own gunner, waited his turn just outside. Now, immediately outside the rear turret of a Lancaster is the Elsan toilet; Jimmy went into such a steep diving turn at high speed that the Elsan became detached from its housing, and deposited its content all over Weasel! No one could go near him for days afterwards, but eventually stores took pity on him, and although it was very difficult in those hard days of 1943 to get any new uniform, they finally decided it would be in everyone's interests if he had a new battledress, and certainly we in the crew of J-Johnnie appreciated it.

June came; the Battle of the Ruhr continued. We flew an air test in the morning three days after the attack on Bochum, quite certain from the order of battle petrol and bomb load that we would be over Happy Valley again that night. We were a few miles south of

Cambridge when we finished our checks, and were about to return to Bourn when we spotted a train steaming towards the city - quite literally "steaming" then, of course. Jimmy dived down towards the last carriage, and we flew alongside the train at about 100 feet. The passengers were obviously enjoying the display as they waved enthusiastically, while the engine-driver and his fireman leaned out of their cabin and gave us a two-fingered Churchillian salute. We climbed and turned and swept back along the other side of the train at low level. We repeated the manoeuvre, then thought it was time to make for base. We landed and taxied round the perimeter track to our dispersal. The Flight Commander's van was there and he was chatting to the ground crew. When Jimmy had shut down the engines and the chocks had been placed in front of the wheels, he strolled over to J-Johnnie. Jimmy slid back the window, and the Wing Commander called up to our pilot, "Jimmy, you're to take a week's kit, and fly up to Scampton directly after lunch." "OK. What for?" "I don't know, you'll get all the gen. when you get there."

Chapter 7

Friedrichshafen-Operation Bellicose
20 June 1943

We didn't object; we would be happy to miss yet another visit to the Ruhr - the target that night turned out to be Cologne, in fact. The Ruhr raids had been going on for two months or more, and losses were increasing. While we had been in Main Force, losses had been about 2.4%; now they were up to 4%, so that on most nights there were usually one or two crews who failed to return. When we got back to the Mess, we soon found that three other crews - Rodley, Sauvage, and Jones - had received similar instructions. We formed a huddle to discuss this development. Our views were ambivalent. On the one hand, we were delighted by the fact that we had received the accolade of being one of a small group selected for something special, while on the other hand we realised that Scampton was the home of 617 Squadron, the Dambusters, whose single operation, exactly a month previously, had cost them eight of the nineteen Lancasters dispatched, a loss rate of 42%. However, it was no more for us to question orders than Tennyson's six hundred, so after lunch we packed a week's kit and flew leisurely northwards till Lincoln Cathedral emerged from the summer haze and moments later we landed at Scampton. Initially it seemed that we were unexpected, but we didn't have to wait long. We were taken to the briefing room by an elderly Group Captain; when I use the term 'elderly,' he was probably all of 35, but we were all in our late teens and early twenties, so he seemed pretty elderly to us. He explained that there was to be a special operation by fifty plus of 5 Group's Lancasters led by the four Pathfinder aircraft, against a special target. Where? He couldn't or wouldn't tell us. When? Soon. That was all he did tell us except that several practices would be held during the next few evenings over Wainfleet Sands, a practice bombing range adjacent to the Wash, and that we were not allowed to go into Lincoln. That was rather disappointing, as everyone in Bomber Command had been stationed near Lincoln at some time or other, and the 'Saracen's Head' was worth revisiting. Sadly, it doesn't exist anymore. However, we consoled ourselves by making up for this in the Mess, and during the evenings flew over the Wash. Two of the Pathfinder crews - P/O Jones and ourselves - illuminated the target at the range with flares, two - Rodley and Sauvage - marked it with TIs, and the main force bespattered it with 11 lb practice bombs. This, it had been decided, would be the plan of attack for the eventual operation, though using something heavier than 11 lb bombs, of course. P/O Jones's navigator, P/O Jimmy Silk DFM, and I became aware that there was considerable onus on us since we would be putting down the first flares.

After a couple of days passed like this - during which I was able to renew contact with Dudley Heal - we were briefed. The target was to be the old airship hangar at Friedrichshafen on Lake Constance, which was being used as an assembly shop for the construction of German radar sets. The Air Commodore in charge of the briefing added that the target was worth bombing from our own point of view, because the radar sets now in the hangar were destined for the Ruhr where they would considerably strengthen the defences. There was a murmur round the room that if he had been to the Ruhr recently, he would realise that the defences certainly didn't need any improvement, and the briefing continued.

The attack was to take place on the first clear night; perfect weather was needed at the target because of its pinpoint nature, very unlike the big areas which had been successfully 'coventrised' in the Ruhr. For the same reason a full or almost full moon was required, so that

FRIEDRICHSHAFEN-OPERATION BELLICOSE

if the attack didn't take place within the next night or two, it would be cancelled altogether. Finally, and almost off-handedly, it was mentioned that Friedrichshafen was much too far into the continent for us to cross the enemy coast in both directions in darkness, so we were to fly south from the target over the Alps, cross the Italian coast just before dawn, and land at one of the newly acquired airfields in North Africa. "Have a good trip, chaps." We spent the afternoon drawing very basic tropical kit from stores, (no one had any badges of rank), preparing maps and charts, and calculating times.

In the evening the weather seemed very good, and we walked optimistically to the Met. Office. The Met. Officer, however, was far from optimistic. He shook his head gloomily. "No, not tonight." The next day passed slowly. We did an air-test, then sat in the mess playing shove-halfpenny. In the afternoon, a preliminary forecast was issued, which promised much better weather conditions than the night before. Eventually news came through: "Operations tonight." We had an operational meal, stowed away navigation equipment, flasks of coffee, and a parcel of sandwiches. The gunners dressed in their Irvines; we strapped on our Mae Wests and parachute harnesses and taxied to the end of the runway.

We took off at 21:40, double British Summer time on the eve of the summer solstice, so there was still ample light. We climbed out of the Lincolnshire mist, and as we gained height we could see other Lancasters climbing from neighbouring airfields. Reading was to be our first turning point, and we remained in a bunch to the coast at Selsey Bill. When we reached the coast, it was much too early, for it would still be light on the other side of the Channel. Sixty Lancasters circled the Bill and fighters from Tangmere, the nearby fighter station, came up and fluttered around inquisitively. Soon, well before I intended to let my pilot set course, one or two more adventurous spirits headed south once more. As the last light faded, we could see the French coast in the distance, and set course. It had long been the custom for southbound aircraft to cross the coast at Cabourg, a little

French seaside resort opposite Le Havre, which I had visited several times before the war when I was on my exchange visits to Normandy. We could always reckon on streams of light flak from the coast, and we were not disappointed; red, green and yellow tracers drifted slowly into the evening air, and extinguished themselves thousands of feet below us. We smiled contemptuously and put our nose down slightly to increase speed by 30 knots to take us through the fighter belt along the French coast.

There was scarcely any wind; navigation was no problem, and the Loire appeared on time. We turned east at Orleans, always very badly blacked out. The weather, which had till then been perfect, now deteriorated; thick cloud above prevented any use of the sextant, and obscured the light from the moon by which we would have seen something of the ground. We didn't worry, however, for an occasional drift taken on a light showed that our track was being made good, and we knew that we should see the Rhine, no matter how bad the weather, and in any case the guns at Mulhouse would probably warn us of its whereabouts. Suddenly there was a shout from Jimmy, "Rhine coming up!" We were fortunately right on time, and right on track. Basle, just to the south, was brilliantly lit up, and we set course for Lake Constance, the Bodensee - the Swiss side as briefed. The Swiss illuminated a few ineffective searchlights and fired a few ineffective shells. The engineer told us the unlikely story of an RT conversation between the pilot of a Flying Fortress and the officer in charge of a Swiss anti-aircraft battery. The Fortress was over Switzerland, probably by mistake since the American navigation was notoriously inaccurate. "You are over Swiss territory. We shall open fire," called the Swiss officer. "I know," called the pilot, and a few moments later, "Your shells are bursting a thousand feet too low." "I know," replied the Swiss officer.

We laughed, and circled the rendezvous point, a small headland, on the Swiss shore of Lake Constance. At Z-4 (ie 4 minutes before the attack was due to begin) we set off across the lake on the agreed

FRIEDRICHSHAFEN-OPERATION BELLICOSE

course, and seconds after crossing the opposite coast, we started releasing flares across Friedrichshafen; moments later a parallel line of flares appeared on our left. The defences were very active indeed; some were accurate too and we could hear shells bursting just below the aircraft; they rocked us about a bit, and shrapnel rattled against the fuselage, but without doing us any real harm. As our last flares fell, a searchlight fastened on to us, and immediately a dozen others held us fast. We twisted and turned frantically, and finally Jimmy dived from 12,000 feet to 2,000 feet out of the target area. Meanwhile the other two Pathfinder aircraft had marked the target with red and green TIs and the Master of Ceremonies was telling the main force aircraft which had been placed most accurately. Soon their bombs were raining down. It was very satisfying because we could see the results of our bombing, something we had rarely seen before; in eighteen visits to the Ruhr, we had seen the ground clearly only twice. We climbed back to lay more flares and add our few small bombs (two 500-pounders) to the general conflagration. Once again the searchlights picked us out from the 60 aircraft circling round - the four Pathfinder planes were flying lower than the main force whom the MC had ordered to climb an extra 5,000 feet because of the intensity of the defences. Once again we were given all the attention of the flak, but this time Jimmy turned hard about and dived out over the lake. Our contribution was complete. Soon the MC pronounced that the raid was at an end and ordered us to climb hard for the Alps.

The Alps were very blue in the summer moonlight; as soon as we had crossed the mountains, we dropped down across the Italian coast and flew low over the Mediterranean. Oxygen masks were taken off; coffee was handed round; the wireless operator picked up some light music. The sun rose; the sea sparkled. We flew just over the wave-tops to escape radar cover. We realised that we were tired, but the excitement of this shuttle-service operation kept us all awake. An occasional smoke-float checked our track, and in two hours the coast appeared...enveloped in thick fog! Early arrivals skimmed the top of the fog leaving a trail behind like the wake of a ship in water. There were frantic voices on the RT: "Ten minutes petrol left!" "I can only fly for a quarter of an hour." It seemed as if a successful operation was going to end in a fiasco; that 420 aircrew would have to bale out, and that 60 Lancasters would be directed out to sea to crash in the Mediterranean when petrol ran out. Fortunately, there was a man of considerable initiative on the ground. He was an American flying control officer who stationed himself at the end of the runway in his jeep, fired Very cartridges up through the mist, and, long before the days of Ground Controlled Approach, talked us in. I shall always remember the expression he used: "The first man to make home base wins!" It was unorthodox, but it was effective; all the aircraft landed safely, about half at Maison Blanche, our intended destination, and the remainder at a neighbouring airfield, Blida. In one of the Lancasters, by coincidence an aircraft from 619 Squadron, which had been formed at Woodhall Spa when we left that station for Bourn, was a dead Bombaimer who had been killed when hit by flak over the target.

For a couple of days we lazed; we drank too much of the rather coarse Algerian wine; we had too much sun; we gorged ourselves on fruit which was now very scarce in England; we bathed in the Mediterranean. One incident while we were there stands out in my mind; we had been issued with basic khaki drill uniform, and none of us had badges of rank except those few who had seen previous service overseas. We ate in an American Mess where one GI was unwise enough to question whether Johnny Sauvage was an officer; Johnny was a very senior Flight Lieutenant at the time, but he was one of those people who nearly always look scruffy because he needed a second shave by about two o'clock in the afternoon; his language at this challenge was picturesque in the extreme, and it obviously served to convince the GI that he really was a 'limey' officer.

Eight of the aircraft which had landed had been too badly damaged on the outward operation to take part in the return one; quite the worst of these was one of the Pathfinder aircraft, Rodley's, not because of

FRIEDRICHSHAFEN-OPERATION BELLICOSE

action over the target, but because a TI had hung up in the bomb-bay of his aircraft; these exploded barometrically, so when he lost height over the Mediterranean, it went off and his Lancaster became filled with smoke and flames; fortunately he realised what had happened, and, opening the bomb doors, he pulled the jettison lever, the TI fell away, and he reached Algiers, but in no fit state to fly again till a good deal of work had been done on his Lancaster. Johnny Sauvage's aircraft was also badly damaged, so there were only two Pathfinders on the return operation. All those who did operate against Spezia, for that was the homebound target, had a great deal of difficulty getting off the ground so heavily laden with petrol and bombs in the heat of a tropical evening.

The homeward attack was something of an anti-climax after Friedrichshafen, and dropping our flares and bombs fairly hastily, we sped back across France. As we got back to Scampton, the sun was rising once more. The WAAF in flying control called us, "Clear to land, J-Johnnie," and for once ignoring RT discipline, "Good show, J-Johnnie." We were debriefed; I recall Jimmy telling the intelligence officer that we 'dove' out of the searchlights; it was years before I found out that 'dove' was legitimate New World past tense of 'to dive.' In the evening we flew back to Bourn.

There was a reception committee waiting for us including the AOC, Bennett, and other senior officers. Bennett was exceedingly angry; he felt that four Pathfinders had been used so that 5 Group would have an excuse, someone else to blame, if the raid were not successful. Relations between Bennett and Cochrane, the AOC of 5 Group, were notoriously bad; Bennett commented at that debriefing that he would have had 20 Pathfinders illuminating and marking the target to ensure that the task was done properly. It was Bennett who had interviewed me for my commission earlier in the year; he didn't waste any time with 'social' questions which some of my friends had suffered from other AOCs but launched straight away into fairly probing questions about navigation, and why I wanted to become an officer; presumably I was able to satisfy him on both counts.

A PATHFINDER IN THE PEENEMÜNDE RAID

The attack on Friedrichshafen had been our 29th operation, and Spezia our 30th, so we got back to Bourn confidently expecting to go on three weeks' leave; the pressure was on, however, and we were informed that we would have to do two more trips before we could be released. We went twice to Cologne before drawing our railway warrants and ration cards and setting off. At that time thirty operations constituted a first tour; one was then entitled to a 'rest' of at least six months before going back for a second tour, though some never did; in Main Force the second tour was twenty operations, but arrangements differed a little in Pathfinder Force. Having got a successful and experienced crew together, Pathfinder Force liked to keep them together for their second tour, so the crew went straight on without a break. In order to compensate for this, the second tour was reduced to 15 operations, and there was a three-week leave period in between instead of the usual two-week end-of-tour leave.

This last operation of our first tour is described in detail in 'Pathfinders at War' by Chaz Bowyer, under the title of 'Night of No Return,' written by Doug Jones, one of the four pilots to take part. There is also quite a long article about it in 'The Marker', the Pathfinder Association magazine, of summer 1991, by Rodley and a shorter one adding to Rod's article by myself in 'The Marker' of winter 1992. I was able to be quite certain of all my details of this operation because I spent a couple of hours of my end-of-tour leave writing it up, since I realised even then that it was a rather special piece of military history. I read quite recently (spring 2002) Constance Babington Smith's 'Evidence in Camera' and was surprised to find how quickly the attack had been organised; Churchill had visited RAF Medmenham, the Photographic Interpretation Unit, on June 14th 1943 and been shown the pictures of the radar devices in preparation at Friedrichshafen; it was only six days later that the raid took place.

FRIEDRICHSHAFEN-OPERATION BELLICOSE

After those two operations against Cologne, which cost the squadron three crews, I didn't go there again for many years, not, in fact, till the autumn of 1998, when my wife and I went down the Rhine on a river cruise starting there. We had not been on the cruise vessel more than ten minutes before there was a fire drill; when it concluded, I said to the Cruise Director, "This is a bit ironic, because the last time I was at Cologne, I was trying to start as many fires as possible!"

Most of our crew had decided to stay together and go on to complete 45 operations; by now we all had great faith in one another, and we all realised that in Jimmy Munro we had an exceptional pilot and captain; Bill Tracey had been absolutely right. (He, Bill, incidentally, had transferred to the US Army Air Corps fairly soon after we had moved to Bourn, and moved on after his thirty operations, so that now, after a long spell together, my friend George, his navigator, moved to a different station.) Two of the crew decided not to stay on: 'Snowy' Nevard, the wireless operator, and Harry Townsley, the engineer. In their place, we picked up two very experienced aircrew; Flight Sergeant Underwood as W/Op., and 'Ginger' Swetman, DFC, DFM, as Engineer. The latter, who eventually became squadron engineering leader, had quite remarkable night vision; he was frequently able to tell intelligence officers at debriefing just where our bombs and TIs had fallen, and time and time again this was confirmed by the photograph taken as we dropped our bombs.

Chapter 8

The Battle of Hamburg-Operation Gomorrah

August 1943

When we got back to Bourn after our three weeks' leave, we found the squadron agog with talk of a new defensive strategy, 'Window', the dropping of metallic strips to confuse the enemy radar. 'Window' was first used against Hamburg on the night of July 24th/25th, 1943, while we were still on leave, and crews who had operated that night told us that the German searchlights and guns were all over the sky, and there was great confusion between the night-fighters and their controllers. The loss rate that night was reduced to 1.5%, only 12 aircraft out of a force of over 700. We then operated against Hamburg three times in a week. On the 27th the loss rate was just over 2%, 18 missing from a force of nearly 800; 'Window' was still being very effective. This particular raid was the night of the great fire-storm; an enormous number of incendiaries was dropped and a great number of the inhabitants of Hamburg perished in the ensuing conflagration. We were back over Hamburg two nights later when the Squadron lost two crews and the Command 28; perhaps the Germans were beginning to get the measure of 'Window'. In the same week we also did a trip to the Ruhr, to Remscheid, so we were operating at quite intense pressure at that time. This was regarded as the end of the Battle of the Ruhr; although the strength of the force was comparatively small - 273 aircraft, whereas all the Hamburg attacks used between 750 and 800 - the operation was particularly concentrated and 83% of the

THE BATTLE OF HAMBURG-OPERATION GOMORRAH

town was devastated. The final 'Battle of Hamburg' raid took place on August 2nd. Although all 97's Lancasters returned, the Command lost 30 aircraft that night - over 4% - but the night's losses were probably due as much to the weather as to the German defences. The icing at 20,000 feet was more severe than we had ever known, and the wind was over 100 knots, so many casualties were certainly the victims of weather.

I pause here from my chronological narrative to insert several anecdotes from this period. One day, we were due to take J-Johnnie on a night-flying test; these normally took place in the morning so that the ground crew could fix anything that needed fixing during the afternoon. For some reason we were not able to fly in the morning - possibly our ground-crew were busy on something fairly major on the aircraft. Whatever the reason, we went for lunch, and arrived to do our air-test early in the afternoon; there was no transport about to take us out to dispersal, so we trooped into the Flight Commander's office to explain. The Wingco said at once, "My van's outside; I shan't be needing it for an hour or two. Take that." Jimmy at once responded that he couldn't drive. W/C Alabaster turned to me and commented, "It makes you realise how long the war's been on, doesn't it? Here's this chap who's done nearly forty trips in a Lancaster and can't drive a car!"

The next story is a sad one. Bennett used to insist that his air staff officers at PFF HQ kept up to date by themselves going on operations from time to time. To my very great surprise, two turned up one evening and both went off with the same crew, an Australian fairly new to the Squadron. I had flown a 'bullseye' with him one night when his own navigator was sick, and, after months flying with Jimmy, wasn't very impressed, so that I wouldn't have wanted to operate with him myself. Sadly both these officers, very experienced officers indeed, were lost with him.

Another story concerns a young night fighter pilot from a Beaufighter Squadron in the Home Counties, who came to spend a week's leave with us and flew on three operations. I was quite amazed that anyone's idea of a week's leave should be to spend it operating with a heavy bomber squadron. Chac'un a son goût! He successfully completed his week, and Jimmy suggested that we would take him back to his base at Twinwood Farm; the main runway at this night-fighter station was considerably shorter than that normally used by a Lancaster, and although we landed without too much difficulty, taking off on an 800 yard runway, skimming over the trees at the end of the runway, was quite exciting. I believe Jimmy got a bit of a rocket when we got back to Bourn, but there isn't really much you can do to a chap who has done 40 operations except perhaps slap his wrists fairly mildly.

By now we were, of course a very experienced crew; when new crews joined the Squadron, their captains were usually sent out with just such a crew before they operated themselves. One night we took a newly arrived South African with us, almost certainly I think to Hamburg. We were making our way over northern Germany, more or less parallel with the coast and were somewhere near Bremen. "Now watch this," said Jimmy and held the plane absolutely straight and level for 30-45 seconds. Then he veered off to the left, and almost immediately three rounds of flak burst on our right, just where we would have been if he had continued straight and level.

Another visitor at about this time was Jimmy's father; he had been in the Canadian army in WW1, and enlisted again as soon as WW2 was declared. Now he was back in England again as Private Munro. By now Jimmy was commissioned, and although Private Munro wasn't allowed to use the Officers' Mess, the Adjutant stretched a point, and accommodated him in the Sergeants' Mess, where he was very well looked after by the NCOs in our crew. He flew with us on an air-test on a very stormy day. While we were out over the North Sea there was a terrific bang, just like a burst of flak directly below the aircraft. We had been struck by lightning! We were lucky; flicking over the pages of Chorley's 'Bomber Command Losses' recently,

THE BATTLE OF HAMBURG-OPERATION GOMORRAH

I noticed that a Halifax which had been struck by lightning broke up in the air, and all the crew were killed. Our only damage was to our main P4 compass; it was never the same again. Although boffins arrived from Farnborough to degauss the aircraft, it could never be relied upon, but fortunately the Distant Reading Compass was still perfectly serviceable, and we relied on that from then on.

We usually went into Cambridge when we were 'stood down' or not flying. (I can recall going into Bourn village only once to go to the Post Office.) The great attraction for me was the Cambridge Arts Theatre, and I used to persuade all the crew to go along quite frequently; they were all quite happy to humour me if a Coward, a Rattigan, a Priestley or an Emlyn Williams was on offer, but they all declined when I suggested a visit to the ballet! We also spent quite a lot of time on the Cam, not in a punt, but in a canoe, for Jimmy, having grown up alongside the Ottawa river, handled a canoe just as expertly as he did a Lancaster.

After what Middlebrook calls 'The Battle of Hamburg' there was a quieter spell. We did two trips to Milan, and between them one to Mannheim where we secured another aiming point picture. In the first of the Milan raids on August 7th, only two planes were lost out of 200 taking part, and on August 12th only three out of 500, and only one of those a Lancaster. I never failed to be surprised at the reactions of some crew members when we were briefed to go on the eight-hour flight over the Alps. They used to complain about these long trips saying, "Why can't we just go to the Ruhr?" Yet they must have known that casualties would be ten or even twenty times as many on a visit to Happy Valley! Moreover there was the joy of flying over the Alps. (A very different experience from flying 15,000 or more feet above the mountains in the well-lit cabin of a modern jet), and long flights posed navigational challenges which I always enjoyed.

Chapter 9

Peenemünde-Operation Hydra
17 August 1943

By now it was the middle of August, and nights were getting longer. The increasing hours of darkness were obviously going to give the C-in-C the opportunity to attack the target he really wanted: Berlin. We thought one morning that the day had come. We always had a look at the Order of Battle when it was published in the morning, not to find which aircraft we were flying in - we knew that - or to find the crew - we knew that too - but to have a look at the information tucked away at the bottom of the sheet, the bomb load and petrol load. These two figures gave a pretty good idea of the vicinity of the target. A small petrol load and a large bomb load almost inevitably meant the Ruhr. Conversely a heavy load of petrol and a small load of bombs probably meant much further afield, Italy or southern or eastern Germany. A moderate load of each would mean Hamburg, Berlin or thereabouts. On August 17th we were scheduled for operations. When we looked at the Order of Battle we were horrified; the petrol and bomb loads appeared just right for Berlin, and yet it was a night of full moon; it would be a massacre - a massacre of the aircraft of Bomber Command by the increasingly skilful Luftwaffe night-fighter crews. There was a general lowering of morale but there was nothing we could do about it so we got on with our air-test, and did some bombing practice as well.

We turned up for afternoon briefing, still feeling rather anxious, and found that although the red tape pinned across the map of Europe on the end wall of the briefing-room stretched out across the North Sea, it stopped short of Berlin. Not Lübeck. Not Rostock. Where? Eventually the target was revealed as Peenemünde, a place none of us had ever heard of. We sat back and waited for more information.

There is no need to write much by way of introduction about the Peenemünde raid. After the Dams operation, it is probably the best documented Bomber Command operation of the whole war. It merits a complete volume to itself by Martin Middlebrook; another by John Searby who was Master of Ceremonies; there are accounts of it and background information in almost any book referring to Bomber Command's activities, notably in R.V. Jones's 'Most Secret War,' in Max Hastings's 'Bomber Command', in Denis Richards' 'The Hardest Victory' and elsewhere. Briefly, Peenemünde was the research station and factory on the coast of the Baltic where the V2 rocket was being developed. It was, of course, a closely guarded secret. Although British intelligence had their first intimations of rockets as early as November 1939, they regarded this as a hoax to distract them from more immediate concerns, until more information came through a Danish engineer in December 1942, and even more when two captured German Generals were 'bugged' in March 1943, and were overheard discussing rocket attacks. Now there was a full alert. The Chiefs of Staff and the War Cabinet were informed, and a decision was made to appoint Duncan Sandys to gather together all possible information. He worked very quickly and used photographic reconnaissance to amplify information which was also now coming in through the Resistance. His report to the War Cabinet was made on June 29th and a decision was made to attack Peenemünde. At first it was thought that Mosquitoes could carry out the attack, but it was realised they couldn't carry the weight of bombs necessary. It would be a job for the heavies, so it was decided to wait until nights were long enough for a force of heavy bombers to get there and back in darkness. Now, in mid-August, that time had come.

A PATHFINDER IN THE PEENEMÜNDE RAID

Briefing took its usual form. There were introductory remarks and the target was finally identified by a senior officer. The Met Officer briefed us on the weather; conditions should be perfect. The Intelligence Officer told us what was known about defences. The Signals Officer briefed us about W/T (Wireless Transmission) procedures and, as always, emphasised the need for radio silence till the attack began. The plan of attack was explained; the operation would be in three phases. (We were to fly in the first.) This first wave was to be against the living quarters of the scientists and technicians; the second against the experimental station and the last against the factory workshops. A number of special features were also explained; there was to be a Master of Ceremonies, the first time such a technique had been employed on a major operation of about 600 aircraft although we had an MC at Friedrichshafen with a much smaller force; there was to be a spoof raid on Berlin by a group of Mosquitoes who would drop 'window' and TIs (Target Indicators) to simulate an impending large-scale raid to attract the German fighters to Berlin. No mention whatsoever was made of rockets; we were told that we would be attacking an experimental radar station, a very important one, but nevertheless, radar was something we knew about. It was only later that we learned about rockets; it was thought that it would be disastrous for British morale if it were known that the Germans were developing rockets, so even the crews were not informed. Finally, we were told, and this was the only occasion I heard such a comment, that if the raid were not successful, it would have to be repeated night after night, irrespective of casualties, till the task was complete. Watches were synchronised. A final word from the senior officer, 'Have a good trip chaps. Wish I were coming with you.' In fact, a very senior officer was with us that night; Group Captain Boyce, Senior Air Staff Officer at Group HQ, turned up and slipped quietly aboard Rodley's aircraft to witness the attack for himself.

We went off to the Mess to have our operational meal, and, of course, made our usual funereal jokes: "Can I have your egg if you're not back tomorrow morning?" I suppose it sounds in very bad taste now, but it was our normal comment to one another; it was really wishing our friends a safe passage, rather like an actor's "Break a leg!" Then I would go to clean my teeth, which by then had become a ritual, and easy enough to undertake because my quarters were between the Mess and the airfield; this had started because I thought that if I were shot down and taken prisoner it might be a long time before I could clean my teeth again! It would have been perfectly simple to carry a toothbrush with me; crew members carried all sorts of things with them. Another ritual was always to wear the silk scarf my mother had given me when I started flying; I would have been very worried to have set off on operations without it.

Meanwhile the armourers had been busy at our aircraft, loading it with a 'cookie', a 4,000-pounder, five 500-pounders, and, most importantly, seven target indicators with which we hoped to mark the living quarters of the most important people at Peenemünde. The petrol bowsers had visited each dispersal site; the ground crew had done their final checks. We went to our lockers in the crew room for our flying kit, and then to the parachute section to draw parachutes, escape kits, rations, and then awaited transport to dispersal. Arriving there, we chatted to the ground crew; the smokers amongst us had a final cigarette; we had a ritual pee over the rear wheel of J-Johnnie.

One such evening while we were waiting at our dispersal point, which was right on the A45, the main road to Cambridge, a coach pulled up; it was carrying an ENSA party, who had performed at Bourn that evening, back to Cambridge. They saw that we were wearing Mae Wests and harnesses and carrying parachutes, so they had asked the driver to stop. They waved and shouted, 'Good luck!' to us, and no doubt read all about the attack - it was on Berlin - in the papers the next morning, so they were able to tell their friends that they had seen a crew just off on a big raid.

We eventually clambered aboard and taxied to the end of the runway, ran up the engines to check magnetos, waited for a 'green' from the controller, and we were off; it was 20:50 DBST, (Double British Summer Time) so it was still light. As usual, there was a little knot of watchers standing at the end of the runway to wave us off. In 'Bomber Command' Max Hastings says that although this happened when the Squadron returned to Coningsby in 1944, there was never a group on the end of the runway at Bourn: not true. I even stood there myself on one or two occasions when I wasn't flying. The point probably was that there was never a big crowd, because the aircraft normally started their take-off run from the eastern end of the main runway, and all the domestic sites were at the western end, so that unless one had transport of some kind - I had a service bicycle at Bourn - it was a very long way to get there.

We flew out over East Anglia in daylight and, as was usual when we were heading east, crossed the coast at Southwold; darkness soon fell as we flew out over the North Sea. It was a beautiful night. The weather was, as forecast, perfect. The sea was calm. There wasn't a cloud in the sky, so as the full moon rose it was shining on the sea in front of us. The occasion was enhanced by the knowledge that we weren't, as we feared we might have been, on our way to the 'Big City'.

It took about an hour and ten minutes to cross the North Sea and reach the Danish coast. We made sure that we kept fairly well north of Flensburg, a spot to avoid when crossing the Schleswig-Holstein peninsula. The flak gunners at Flensburg were both trigger-happy and accurate, and whenever we went that way, there always seemed to be some unfortunate character whose navigator had not kept him clear of that city. In fact, as we approached the coast of Denmark, we saw that there was someone ahead of us in trouble, serious trouble. An aircraft was coned and flak was bursting around it; suddenly there was an enormous explosion, and a ball of fire fell towards the earth. I must have been very callous at that age, because rather than feeling sorry for the crew I thought, "An aircraft ahead of us must be another Pathfinder, and what in heaven's name is a Pathfinder navigator doing being so incompetent as to stray so far off track into such a heavily

PEENEMÜNDE-OPERATION HYDRA

defended area?" There were obviously times when you just had to go through the defences - nearly every time you crossed the target area, for example - but I saw no point in doing so unnecessarily. It was the only aircraft we saw shot down that night, most unusual.

We crossed Denmark in less than fifteen minutes and turned southeast over the multitude of islands in the Baltic, which made navigation very easy. I gave Jimmy and Sus the Estimated Time of Arrival, and just as that time was coming up, there was a shout from the bomb-aimer that there was a smoke screen ahead of us and he couldn't see very much at all. I came from behind my curtain, and he was quite right! I could see very little, but this was from a fairly oblique angle; there appeared to be 100% cover of the target, but as we got nearer and were looking down through the smokescreen more vertically, it became obvious that cover was by no means complete, and that one could see quite a lot down through the lines of smoke. Defences were very meagre; a few searchlights straggled round the sky; we had no problem dropping our bombs and TIs on time. The attack seemed to have started well. We watched for a few moments and then turned away from the target just south of the inward route of those still approaching, again making sure that we kept well away from Flensburg. We flew back across the North Sea thinking that losses would be negligible. Our return to Bourn was uneventful; 97 Squadron had sent out 18 aircraft; one returned early with engine trouble; the other 17 all landed safely. Our flight had lasted 6 hours 50 minutes.

We had a quick word with the ground crew, then transport arrived to take us back to the flight offices. First, we went to the parachute store, then to the crew room to deposit our harnesses and other flying kit, and so to the ops. room for debriefing. As usual there was a senior officer waiting to have a word with us as we went in and took a mug of coffee from a WAAF (with rum in it for those who wanted it, which always included the half-frozen gunners, of course), then on to an intelligence officer waiting to debrief us. We sat around a table with him, and told him about the raid, the defences, any aircraft we had seen shot down, the weather; it didn't take long before we were on our way back to our messes for the traditional post-operational meal of eggs and bacon and trimmings. And so, to bed.

The next morning, as on every morning after operations, I was about early. Most of the crew, most of the squadron would sleep in till lunchtime after flying at night, but probably I was horrified at the thought of missing a meal, so I was always up. I wouldn't pretend I was first in the mess for breakfast, but I would be up by about eight, have a shower, and reach the mess just before breakfast ended at nine. After breakfast, I would normally catch up with my correspondence, or do the Telegraph crossword, and read the paper or a novel; on this particular occasion, however, realising that the previous night's operation had been rather a special one, and with the threat made at the end of briefing still hanging over us, I decided to walk up to the intelligence library to have a look at the photographs which had, no doubt, been developed. The first thing I found was that we had lost 40 aircraft, 6.7% of the force. I was amazed; the only aircraft we saw downed was the one over Flensburg; usually we saw at least half a dozen over German targets. Apparently, the German fighters had circled Berlin as they were intended to, but when their controllers realised where the target really was, they redirected the fighters to the Baltic coast, and they arrived in time to create havoc among the later waves of the attack. The second wave suffered losses of about 14.5%, while the third, the Lancasters of 5 Group, lost almost 20%, an incredible one aircraft in every five. However, the raid had been deemed a success, so we should not have to repeat it, much to our relief. The attack is said to have delayed the V2 by about three months. The first V2 hit London on September 8th, 1944, and three months before that, almost to the day, the invasion was just getting under way, so we probably did something worthwhile. Reports tell of several top scientists and technicians who were killed; production was dispersed and considerably decreased. The German general in charge of fighters committed suicide after failing to defend Peenemünde.

Chapter 10

Berlin – End of Tour

August–September 1943

This operation was our 40th. We had five more to do. We did air-tests on August 19th and 22nd but didn't operate again till the 23rd. The full moon had passed, and now it really was Berlin. We lost 56 aircraft, Bomber Command's biggest loss in a single operation to date, 7.9% of the force despatched. One of the aircraft we lost that night was the Australian with two Staff Officers on board. Four nights later, we went to Nuremberg; the nights really were getting longer now, which enabled us to go that far under cover of darkness; there was much evidence of aerial combat, but fortunately the fighters left us alone. On the 29th we flew over to Oakington, our parent station, to operate from there while our runways at Bourn were under repair, and on the night of 30th/31st August went back to the Ruhr, to München-Gladbach, a flight of only 3hrs 30 minutes. Take-off that night was after midnight, and by 20:20 the same evening we were back in the air on our way to Berlin. Losses were again high; 47 aircraft, 7.6%, but much higher among the Stirlings which lost 17 out of 106 sent, 16.0%. We lost one of our Flight Commanders, Wing Commander Burns, CO of A flight, with his much-decorated crew. Fortunately, he and a number of others of his crew escaped the aircraft and were taken prisoner. He had been Master Bomber over Berlin in the raid a week before.

We were now in September with one trip left to complete our second tour. We did night-flying tests on two occasions, but each time operations were cancelled through bad weather. On the first of these occasions, the corporal-fitter in charge of J-Johnnie, a young married man, was due to go on leave the next morning, but when operations were 'scrubbed' he wouldn't go; the same happened the next night; he was determined to see us safely through our tour. This was a considerable sacrifice, for ground crew got very little leave, and worked outside at dispersal sites, not in a warm hangar, in sometimes quite atrocious conditions; he really deserved an award for devotion to duty. I was glad that Jimmy saw the Flight Commander the next morning before we all set off on leave, explained what had happened, and the Wingco extended the corporal's leave, which officially had already started, by a 48-hour pass, a most unusual concession for those days.

We had expected a 'cushy' operation to Italy for that final operation; the petrol/bomb load on the Order of Battle seemed right for a long trip, and the invasion of Italy had begun that very morning, September 3rd, the fourth anniversary of the outbreak of war. We were soon disillusioned when we got to briefing; once more the red tape stretched across Europe to Berlin, but by a particularly long circuitous route, which accounted for the bomb and petrol loads. We went through the usual pre-operation routines, but when Jimmy was running up the engines on the end of the runway, the surge of power made all my radar unserviceable; not, I thought, a good omen for our last operation. However, our luck was in once again, for even at 20,000 feet the winds were quite light and variable that night, so we had no real navigational problems. We got a pin-point on the English coast, another on the Dutch, and the rear gunner was able to give me an occasional drift, so, even by that circuitous route, we got to the target successfully. The Halifaxes and Stirlings did not participate in this operation, as they had recently suffered severe losses; 316 Lancasters passed through the target in 20 minutes hoping to overwhelm the German defences of their capital. Even so 22 were lost, nearly 7% of the force. A year earlier, Bomber Command could hardly have sent 100 Lancasters, even on a 'maximum effort.'

BERLIN – END OF TOUR

We were routed over the southwestern corner of Sweden for the return flight. Martin Middlebrook's book on the Berlin raids refers to the correspondence between the Swedish Ambassador and Anthony Eden, Foreign Secretary during the war. In his reply to the Ambassador's protest about the 'repeated violations of Swedish territory,' Eden wrote, 'On returning from their target, a number of aircraft took a northerly course and, despite the instructions which, as Your Excellency knows, have been issued to British air crews to avoid flying over Swedish territory, crossed the Southwest corner of Sweden before reaching the Kattegat.' Sheer hypocritical nonsense, of course; our briefing lay down the route for the return journey.

As we crossed the corner of Sweden, we put the nose down and, for the last time, sped home. Despite having no radar, we were easily first home that night. As we crossed the coast, we broke discipline by firing off the colours of the day from the Very pistol. When we got back to the parachute section, I pulled the ripcord of my parachute, which I wouldn't normally have done, of course, and it spilled over the counter. The WAAF parachute packer and I had a laugh about it, when I said that I was satisfied that it would have been all right if I had had to use it in earnest.

The next day, the BBC News Bulletins included an account of the operation by Wynford Vaughan Thomas, a reporter who had been in one of the Lancasters. He didn't mention the return route over Sweden.

After completing my log-book for this final operation, I added a brief statistical analysis at the back of the book. Our 45 operations had occupied 289 hrs 5 mins flying time. We had transported to the Third Reich and its satellites one eight-thousand-pound bomb, 37 four-thousand-pounders, 58 one-thousand-pounders, 53 five-hundred-pound bombs, 74 Target Indicators, 17,690 four-pound incendiary bombs, as well as smaller numbers of mines, flares, 250-pounders, thirty-pound incendiary bombs and, of course, leaflets. While we were with 97, twenty-six crews had been lost from the Squadron, exactly half of those during raids in which we had participated.

The following day we set off on a fortnight's leave. The possibility of surviving the war, although by no means certain, seemed considerably nearer.

Sadly, Jimmy, Ron Bennett, and 'Weasel' did not survive; they, with our new wireless operator, Flight Sergeant 'Gremlin' Underwood, Jimmy Silk, from Doug Jones's crew, who replaced me, Peter Burbridge, from Johnny Sauvage's crew who replaced 'Sus', and a new engineer, were shot down over Berlin on the night of November 22nd/23rd 1943, probably by a German fighter. They have no known grave. It was Jimmy's 57th operation.

What must have been the next J-Johnnie was not destined to last very long; it was shot down and all its crew killed on the night of 30th/31st January 1944 returning from Berlin. I was, by then, many miles from Bourn, and was not to know about this for many years. However, in 1999, BBC Leeds made a programme about the recovery of the remains of the aircraft by Dutch engineers excavating at Zwanenburg. The programme did seem to include a number of anomalies, and I had a brief correspondence with the Research Assistant working on the programme, but she was unable to resolve my enquiries and pointed out, quite correctly, that the programme was really about the excavation, not the minutiae of 97 Squadron's history. I had not known before the programme was shown that it was to be about OF (97 Squadron's identification letters) - J-Johnnie, only that it was to be about a Lancaster; it therefore gave me quite a frisson to be watching a programme about OF-J, an aircraft with the identical identification to the one which I had myself been navigating only a few months before.

Taunton's schoolboys making their way to Southampton station in 1939 on their way to evacuation in Bournemouth, and including Doctor King, English teacher, and future Speaker of the Commons.

Heinkel 111 brought down by PAC at Watton, February 18th 1941

On the way to Iceland

Above and opposite top: The RAF Transit Camp 17km from Reykjavik

Hot springs near the camp

Lakeland School of Aeronautics, Florida

The flight line, Stearman PT-13s

Five of us with Bill Lethio, our instructor

Bob, Ginger and Cyril in U.S. Air Corps "fatigues". Bob later became Sqdn/Ldr R.G.Knight, DSO., DFC. with 617 Squadron

Pensacola, the weekly letter home

Pensacola, practising astro-navigation

Course 1A-P-(BQ) leaves Pensacola, May 1942

Pensacola: more - very relaxed - astro practice

Flight Plan for ferry-delivery of Ventura from Gander, Newfoundland, to Prestwick, Scotland, May, 1942

L.A.C.s Finney, Spencer, Manning and Stephens at No. 3 A.F.U., Bobbington, August, 1942

Above left: Sergeants Jimmy Munro and Arthur Spencer on leave at Southampton from OTU

Above right: P.O. Spencer at Southampton, August, 1943

Below: The original crew of J-Johnnie at Woodhall Spa, January 1943. Harry Townsly, 'Snowy' Nevard, Eric Suswain, Jimmy Munro, 'Weasel' Hill, Arthur Spencer, and Rob Bennett, then all Sergeants.

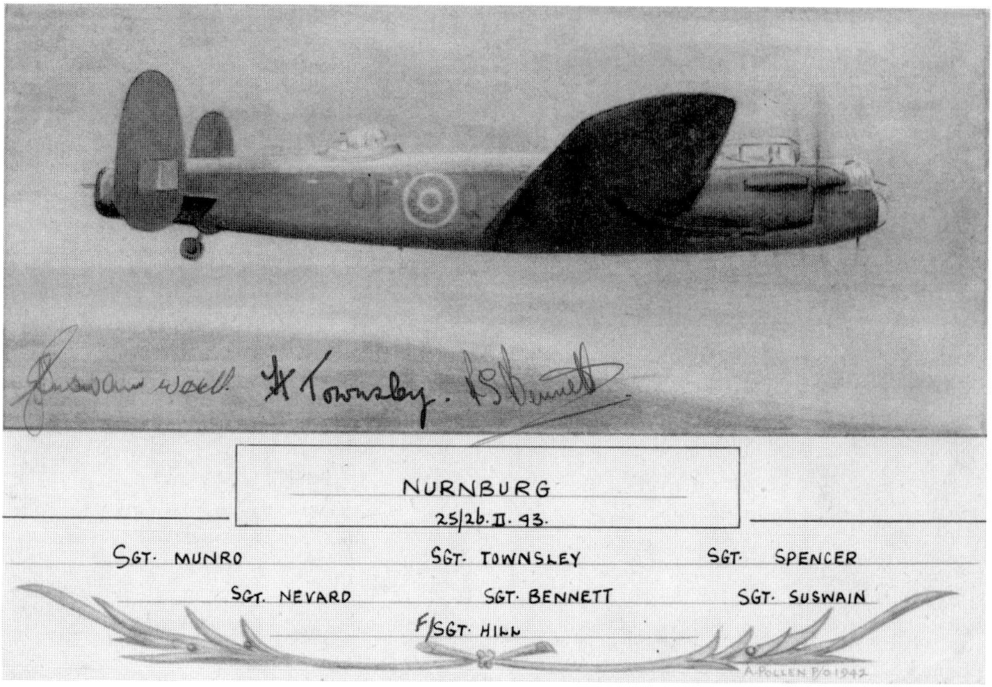

Certificate awarded by 5 Group to crew for aiming-point photo in operation against Nuremberg, February 1943

Certificate awarded by 5 Group to crew for aiming-point photo in operation against St. Nazaire, March 1943

Certificate awarded by 5 Group to crew for aiming-point photo in operation against Milan, February, 1943

Certificate awarded by 5 Group to crew for aiming-point photo in operation against Lorient, February. 1943

OF-J-Johnnie and crew just before bombing-up with TIs

Crew and ground crew and a 'cookie' in front of J-Johnnie, August 1943

Jimmy and the gunners at Bourn, September 1943

Some of the crew and ground-crew, September 1943

(Left to right) Underwood, Suswain, groundcrew, Bennett, Spencer, groundcrew, Hill, Munro, groundcrew, groundcrew in front of J-Johnnie (note the increasing line of bombs) at Bourn, August 1943

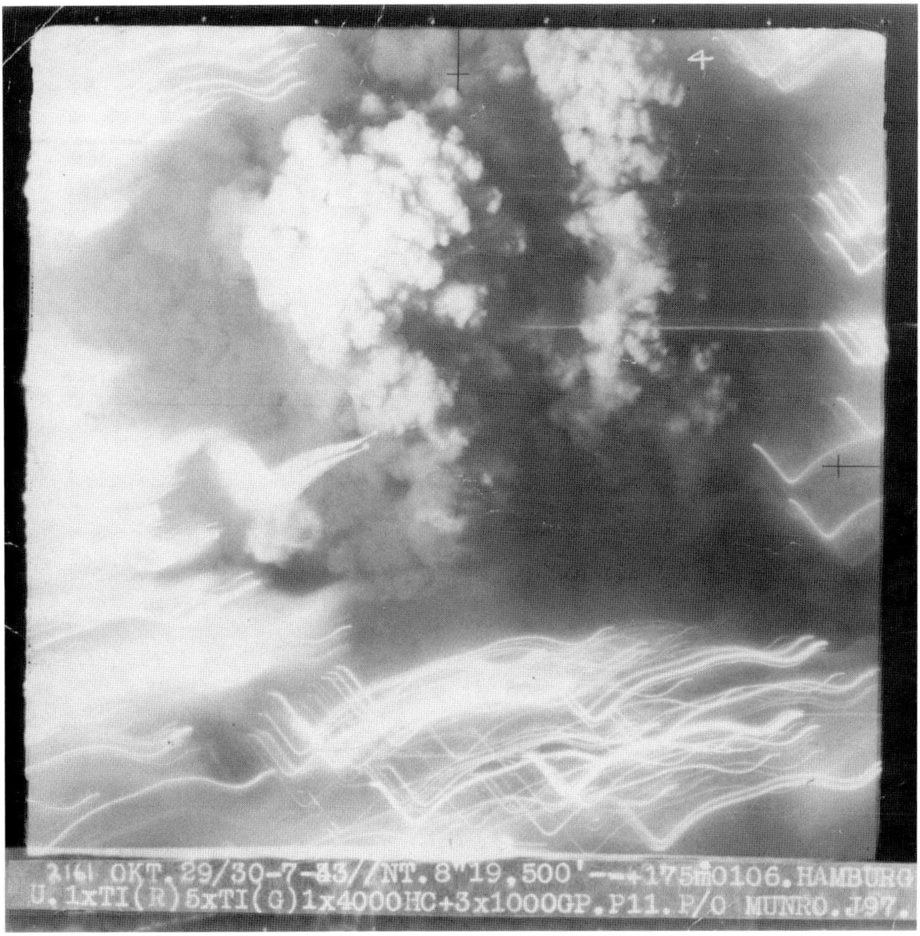

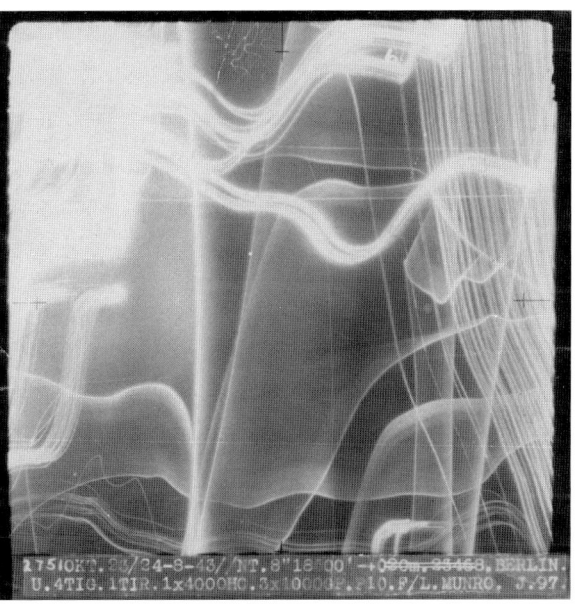

Above and right: Over Hamburg, 29 July, and Berlin, 23 August, 1943, from J-Johnnie. Notice Jimmy's deservedly rapid promotion

Above: In front of my tent at El Adem, near Tobruk, February, 1944

Below: At Celone, near Foggia, Italy, April 1944

Right: In front of Brandenburg Tor, Berlin during Operation Plainfare, the Berlin Airlift, August, 1949.

Chapter 11

The Mediterranean Theatre Part 1
December 1943–July 1944

I left 97 Squadron at Bourn on September 23rd 1943, posted to No.26 OTU at Wing, just outside of Leighton Buzzard, as a navigation instructor. I hadn't been there many weeks when a notice appeared in Daily Routine Orders seeking a radar navigation instructor overseas. With the Middle East and North Africa now in allied hands, it was pretty obviously going to be Italy. I hadn't really settled to life as an instructor after life on an operational squadron; moreover, the post was 'advertised' as a Flight Lieutenant vacancy, and since I hadn't been commissioned all that long, I asked the Adjutant to put my name forward. It wasn't long before I heard that I had been accepted and went off on embarkation leave. On my return the unit was good enough to divert a cross-country to drop me off at Squire's Gate, Blackpool, where the embarkation unit was based. Within days I was on a ship bound for overseas from Liverpool, but conditions were rather different this time as I was travelling as an officer, and in any case the vessel was hardly a traditional troopship. We sailed well out into the Atlantic to keep clear of the aircraft attacking convoys from airfields in western France, then turned east to pass through the Straits of Gibraltar, where the fog was so dense that although the Straits are very narrow, nine miles at its narrowest, we saw no signs of the Rock whatsoever and a couple of days later docked in Algiers.

After a day or two in a transit camp there, I was flown to Tunis, Headquarters of Mediterranean Air Command, to which I was attached for the time being. The Air Officer Commanding was Air Marshal Tedder; he would come into the Mess occasionally, and was a delightful man; in fact, I never met any really senior officers who were not very pleasant people indeed. The more objectionable men were those pre-war regular officers, who had probably never operated during the war and got stuck at about Group Captain or Air Commodore level, were never going to get any further, and many of whom were far less attractive personalities than people like Tedder, who really did get to the top.

I was looked after by a Wing Commander and a Squadron Leader. It was now mid-December, and they took a light aircraft to Bône (now known as Annaba, Algeria) one day to visit the market. They took me along with them, since I was under their wing, and because they had found out that my French was fairly reasonable. They had hoped to find some turkeys for the mess for Christmas but were unlucky; all we did get was a sack of carrots, but probably it was appetising for people who had lived on service rations for some time to have some fresh vegetables.

While at Tunis, I did manage to visit the site of Carthage, and a WAAF officer and I had a swim in the Mediterranean on Christmas Day; it really was fairly chilly, but we wanted to say that we had swum on Christmas Day!

A few days after Christmas, I set off further east to El Adem, a large desert airfield just outside Tobruk. I had learnt while I was at Tunis that the bomber squadrons, mainly Wellingtons, but one Halifax, No. 462, which had come up through the desert, and had spent much of the war raiding places like Benghazi and Tobruk, were shortly to move across to Italy, and that one of the squadrons, the Halifaxes, was going to become a target marking force, doing the same sort of job that I had been doing in Pathfinder Force. Indeed, one of their crews had been sent back to England to undertake the Pathfinder course with 8 Group at Upwood, and had flown one operation with Bomber Command before returning to the Mediterranean theatre.

THE MEDITERRANEAN THEATRE PART 1

I spent initially only a few days with them before being required to visit HQ Middle East Air Force at Cairo, the HQ which, through 205 Group, had much more direct control over this bomber force than the HQ at Tunis. There were aircraft continuously going through El Adem on their way to the Far East, so a lift was once again arranged for me in a Wellington. Since the Wellington had its own crew I stood in the astrodome throughout the flight; I recall how impressed I was as we approached the Nile Delta at the sharp demarcation between the sands of the desert and the green of the delta, not a gradual change at all, but quite sudden. The sergeant-pilot levelled out at about thirty or even thirty-five feet above the runway at Cairo West, then dropped the aircraft in with a terrific bang. Since I had been in the astrodome, not the warmest place in the aircraft, I was wearing a flying jacket; as I left the Wellington a Wing Commander approached me outside flying control and asked if I were the pilot of the aircraft which had just landed; since I had my flying jacket on, he could not, of course, see what sort of a brevet I was wearing. I very hastily disclaimed such responsibility and commented that I could quite understand why he was asking. He grinned and went off to find the real pilot.

I spent several days at HQ Middle East seeing a succession of fairly senior officers, most of whom had been in the Middle East for some time, and were not in close touch with recent developments in Bomber Command. One of them also introduced me to the delights of Groppi's, the famous Egyptian tea rooms, where one could gorge oneself on the sort of cakes that hadn't been seen in England for years.

Soon I was back at El Adem where 462 Squadron were still carrying out an occasional night raid on German harbour installations in Crete, but everyone was really just waiting for the move to Italy. Towards the end of February, all the ground crew moved back to the Delta to be ferried across to Italy to prepare an airfield near Foggia for the arrival of the Halifaxes. We kept our tents for the moment, but the khamsin was beginning to blow, and there was sand in everything.

Occasionally a very old, quite enormous - and very dirty - Arab riding a donkey far too small for him would appear carrying a bucket of tiny eggs, which he would barter for a mug of sugar. The last night we were there, the tents were taken down and stowed aboard the aircraft for an early departure; we slept under the wings of the Halifaxes. I flew with the Squadron CO as navigator, since he had no regular crew of his own. The Engineering Officer (ground) flew as his flight engineer, so we had rather a makeshift crew. However, we reached Celone, our designated airfield, without problems. Just before we left the desert, I went into Tobruk and bought a pair of gumboots at the Officers' Shop; you were allowed to buy gumboots only if you were to be posted to Italy; it didn't seem as if we were going to have very wonderful weather in Italy!

During the next few weeks, I spent most of my time with the squadron Navigation Officer and his team, some airborne on long cross-countries, talking to them about the techniques we had used in Pathfinder Force and the equipment we used, 'which in their case they had not got' (slightly adapting the Henry Reed poem referred to earlier). An entry in my log-book for May 2nd 1944, shows the first air test of the Italian Gee chain; it was, of course, going to be an enormous advance for crews which had come up through the desert with no such aids to have Gee available, but they would certainly need it over the coming months for weather over Europe was very different from weather along the North African coastline.

At about this time, I was posted from 462 Squadron to HQ 205 Group as Group Navigation Officer (Radar) to distinguish me from the Group Navigation Officer; the work involved quite a lot of visits to HQ 15th Air Force, which was based at Bari, and under whose aegis 205 Group operated. 462, now for some reason rechristened 614 Squadron, started operating in their new role. Their first attempt was something of a fiasco, not through any fault of theirs, but because the chosen target was in Sofia, and the mountains all round prevented their new radar devices from operating effectively; this was a pity, because it took them some time to win back their credibility with the supporting bomber squadrons.

One morning in June, news broke of the invasion of Normandy; the unit sick quarters had a radio, and I stood outside most of that morning (sick quarters being in a tent) and listened to the commentators, rather wishing that I had a hand in these great events taking place the other side of Europe.

Another event at about this time was the eruption of Vesuvius; a stream of smoke spread east from the crater over Italy, right across the plain around Foggia, where all the main airfields were. We had to send out a navigation warning to all squadrons not to fly into the smoke from the volcano since it would damage the perspex in the cockpits of their aircraft.

Chapter 12

Valence la Trésorie

24 July 1944

It wasn't long before I got the urge to go along with 462/614 from time to time. I knew only too well that Bennett had insisted on his Air Staff Officers operating in order to keep them in touch with current techniques, and now that I was a Staff Officer myself, albeit a very junior one, I thought I ought to do the same; moreover I was well aware of Hotspur's castigation of Staff Officers in Henry IV, and Siegfried Sassoon's poem about 'scarlet majors at the base,' so I decided I would join the squadron if there were appropriate opportunities. By 'appropriate opportunities' I mean providing I could go as a crew member; I knew only too well how much some crews hated having an 'extra bod.' on board as a supernumerary. Moreover, having completed forty-five operations, I thought it would be nice to make the round figure of fifty.

There was a meeting of the Air Staff every morning, which I attended. It was also attended by an army officer, a Guard, attached to the Group HQ, who was responsible for liaison with the Resistance, both in France and in Yugoslavia. He arrived one morning to inform us that the French Resistance intended to attack an airfield in the Rhône Valley in the near future; they would be doing this at night and would welcome a diversion by bomber aircraft making an attack on the middle of the airfield to make the Germans keep their heads down while they went about their business around the perimeter. This sounded a very interesting trip. I contacted 614 Squadron and found there was one crew without a navigator; by coincidence the same crew with whom I had undertaken the initial test of the Italian Gee chain. They were quite happy to accept my suggestion that I should join them for this operation as navigator. I got to Celone in ample time to renew acquaintance with Flt Lt Langton and his crew, and to be present at briefing, though I had all the information needed already, of course.

The front line at this time ran roughly from Ancona across Italy, just north of Florence. We were not routed to cross the line, but flew north as far as Lake Trasimeno, now, I believe, more commonly known as Lake Perugia; I prefer the former since that was the site of one of Hannibal's battles in the Punic Wars. We took off at about twenty to seven and set course for the lake; the date was July 24th, about three weeks before the invasion of southern France on August 15th. We turned west when we reached the Lake, and crossed the coast near Livorno, Leghorn. We crossed the Ligurian Sea, pinpointed the northern tip of Corsica and crossed the French coast near Marseilles, then north again along the valley of the Rhône as far as Valence. The airfield we were to attack was close to Valence; we were given its name as La Trésorie, but although I've looked it up in several reference books about the resistance since the war, I've never found anything about an airfield of that name. We dropped our flares and one TI from about 10,000 feet and watched while the main force, mainly Liberators, bombed the centre of the airfield. There was obviously some activity on the ground, small arms fire and a number of explosions. There seemed to be no defences whatsoever. The attack over, we turned about, and flew back to Foggia by the same route. I added a further 8 hours 5 minutes operational flying in my logbook.

A fortnight later, on August 6th, the Army liaison officer announced at our morning meeting that a message had now been received from the Resistance in southern France. They had been well satisfied with the diversion provided, had destroyed 37 German aircraft on the ground, had blown up the ammunition dump, and killed an unspecified number of Germans.

Many years later, at about the time of my retirement, I began to wonder what were the details of what had happened on the ground that night. Initially I wrote to the town archivist at Valence, but received no reply. A French friend then suggested that I wrote to the Société des Anciens Combattants. The Secretary responded quite quickly by sending a copy of the report of the local Director of what we know as Air Raid Precautions - ARP. This was interesting - reporting one or two casualties to civilians and to cattle - but not quite what I wanted; were there not perhaps among her members those who were personally involved in this operation? Eventually she put me in touch with two members, but one denied that any such RAF raid had taken place, while the other claimed that the Resistance was so much on the defensive, that they could not possibly have mounted an attack on the German airfield. My son-in-law, who was undertaking much research at the time at The National Archives in connection with his book, "Black Night for Bomber Command", carried out some investigation, as did a friend of his who was well acquainted with that part of the Rhône Valley. Neither was able to find the sort of information I wanted. We seemed, like Churchill, to have come up against the politics of the French Resistance. ("We all have our cross to bear, and my cross is the Cross of Lorraine".) Some years later, I was attending an RAF Historical Society conference on the theme of the war in the Northern Mediterranean 1944-45, and explained my predicament to Dr N.S. Ritchie, a member of the Air Historical Branch of the RAF. He wrote to me a few weeks later suggesting that 'resistance movements were of course notorious for grossly exaggerating their exploits. They assumed that by doing so they would ensure that they received ample Allied support in the form of supplies, etc., in future.'

I navigated twice more for 614 Squadron. One operation was a long trip to Hungary, to Székesfehérvár, halfway between Lake

Balaton and Budapest, the other to the marshalling yards at Zagreb in northern Yugoslavia; the aim of both these trips was to impede the Germans as they retreated from the Balkans and on each occasion we carried fifteen small bomb containers, each holding six flares. Two of the Group's aircraft were lost on the visit to Hungary, while we returned from Zagreb on three engines. It occurred to me much later that apart from the single operation undertaken by the crew sent back to the UK for Pathfinder training, I was probably the only person to have flown both in Pathfinder Force, and the Target Marking Force operating from Italy!

I did two more operations in Wellingtons, which were now much involved in supply dropping to the partisans. I thought that these would prove interesting and arranged to navigate for a crew without a navigator in 40 Squadron. The first was in daylight, high in the mountains near Sarajevo; the partisans, looking like a gang of bandits, waved with great enthusiasm as our parachutes floated down to them. The same evening, we dropped from 1,000 feet on to an enormous bonfire in the form of a cross near Trieste.

Chapter 13

The Mediterranean Theatre Part 2

July 1944–December 1944

Life was not all operations and staff work, however; in August I was given the opportunity to undertake a Junior Commander's course at HQ Middle East in Cairo. I flew to Cairo via Malta and Marble Arch - a rather more pleasant flight than my previous trip to Cairo - and spent an interesting four weeks living on a houseboat, where the course also took place. The boat was moored to Gezira Island, and we were able to use the facilities at the club there in our fairly ample leisure time. Before I was allowed to return to Foggia, HQ ME sent me off to give a couple of lectures to navigators at their bomber OTU at Qastina and their Heavy Conversion Unit at Abu Sueir on the techniques and equipment used in Pathfinder Force. And so back to Foggia, this time via El Adem, now very much a backwater, and Malta.

Most of the staff visits I undertook from Foggia were to Bari, the Headquarters of the American 15th Air Force, but on one occasion I visited HQ MATAF (Mediterranean Allied Tactical Air Forces) at Sienna. Most of the day I was there was in an office with RAF and USAAC officers, but we did find time to walk round the great square; I thought what a wonderfully attractive place it was, and how I would love to go back there; in fact, it was a great many years before I returned on a day when the weather was appalling and the square was packed almost solid with tourists, so that my wife wasn't nearly as impressed as I had been almost fifty years earlier, when the sun shone, the sky was blue, and there was no one about but a few Allied troops.

I also visited MAAF HQ at the great palace at Caserta, and while there was able to ascertain the whereabouts of my first RAF friend, Ken Romain, who I knew was flying with a Spitfire squadron. They were stationed, in fact, quite nearby, so I was able to spend an enjoyable afternoon and evening with these fighter boys. They went off for a sweep over the front line while I was there. In their Ops. Room (a caravan), I noted that Ken had been credited with one half of a "kill". I pulled his leg about this, pointing out that all the time I had been flying over Germany, he had shot down one half of a Luftwaffe aircraft. However, he protested - and I am sure he was right - that Allied air superiority had been so great over North Africa, and now was over Italy, that opportunities for combat were very rare; when they were patrolling the front line, the German aircraft just did not leave the ground.

By now, my job in the Mediterranean theatre was just about over. The Target Marking Squadron was well able to look after itself. (During the autumn one of the new crews to join them was captained by an Old Tauntonian from Southampton, R.G.Wilson. He was slightly younger than me but was an accomplished games player, so I had known him quite well; he was given a permanent commission, and was a regular member of the RAF cricket XI for several years; when he retired as a Group Captain he became Secretary of Notts CCC. We were planning to do an op. together when I was posted back to the UK.) It was early December when I left Foggia. The Group Communications Flight took me across to Naples, and from there I was taken on by the USAAC Transport system. I had a couple of days at Marseilles en route and then went on to Paris. Arriving at Orly, I enquired of the American movements sergeant if there was any chance of breaking my journey in Paris for 24 hours: "Sure, sir." I have the impression that the Americans were much more relaxed about such things; I would never have got away with that if I had been travelling with Transport Command. He probably thought I wanted a night out in Paris, and so I did, but not perhaps quite the sort of night he imagined. What I wanted to do was to look up the family I had known before the war, and find out about the friends of whom I had heard nothing since the collapse of France in 1940. I found a phone, and much to my surprise, the civil telephone system was working perfectly satisfactorily. I contacted my friends, spent a very pleasant evening with them, and was able to hear all about my acquaintances in Normandy.

Monsieur Hue, the father of the family, told a delightful story about an incident during the occupation. He had been strap-hanging on the Metro, when a German officer alongside him took out his cigarette case and lighter and was about to light a cigarette; M Hue touched him on the arm and pointed to the notice. "Défense de fumer, Monsieur," he said. The German officer put away his cigarette and lighter. Monsieur Hue turned to me, obviously absolutely delighted. "Petite victoire," he said, "petite victoire!"

Chapter 14

Transport Command
January 1945–December 1945

When I reached the UK I was sent on leave, during which I was able to organise a visit to HQ Pathfinder Force, where I still had some contacts. I spent a most interesting evening in the Ops. Room reacquainting myself with all the latest developments including particularly the use of Mosquitoes as the Light Night Striking Force; I spent a second evening with Wing Commander Burns DSO DFC who had been shot down over Berlin just before I left Bourn and lost a hand when he was blown out of his Lancaster; he had been in hospital the next two nights in Berlin when further big raids took place; not a pleasant experience he had assured me! Eventually he had been repatriated through Switzerland, the normal procedure for badly injured servicemen, though his injuries did not prevent him doing a worthwhile job as an Air Staff Officer at 8 Group Headquarters.

I was just beginning to think the RAF had forgotten all about me when I received a signal to report to a certain Wing Commander at Adastral House, the Headquarters of the Air Ministry in London. After a few minutes introductory chatter, he asked what I wanted to do now. This surprised me as it wasn't the usual service way of doing things; I must have looked a bit perplexed, for he went on, "What about going to Transport Command?" I certainly had no objections to this, so he sent me off on leave again to await instructions. Eventually, sometime in February, I received instructions to report to the Transport Command OTU at Bramcote in the Midlands.

Although the vast majority of air crew arriving for the OTU course were very experienced, Transport Command saw fit to give us a very thorough training, especially in navigation and meteorology; the course in the latter was one of the best I had ever done. One of the advantages of the course was that if one got a certain percentage in the end-of-course examinations and took an extra paper in civil aviation law one could qualify for a First Class Air Navigator's Licence, which would enable one to fly in civil aviation. We also did quite a lot of cross-country flying in Wellingtons, there being a surfeit of them at the time. There were only three of us in a Transport Command crew; pilot, wireless operator and navigator. I crewed up with an ex Spitfire pilot, and a wireless operator who had, in fact, flown in one of the Wellington Squadrons of 205 Group in the desert.

There was another rather more important piece of "crewing up" while I was at Bramcote, for I met my wife; she was a theatre staff nurse at Nuneaton General Hospital, where she had done her training; we were married not all that long after we first met. Our daughters sometimes tease us about that even now!

At the end of the course, we were posted to a Ferry Unit at Talbenny, which is beyond Haverfordwest at the far south-western corner of Wales. On the way there by train, I had to wait about four hours in Gloucester, where I arrived at about 7 in the evening. I went along to the nearest hotel for a meal. When I went in, the Manager was in reception and asked, "Are you with the team, sir?" I must have looked as perplexed as I felt, for he went on immediately to explain that a cricket match in preparation for the forthcoming "Victory" Test series between Australia and England was starting the next day at the Gloucestershire cricket ground, and that both sides were staying at his hotel. The two sides had a room booked for the evening for some social activity, and since I appeared to be the only other Air Force officer in the hotel, they invited me to join them. I had a most jolly evening with them; many of those present are now household names in the cricketing world; the Australians were captained by Warrant

Officer Lindsay Hasset; the side included Keith Miller and other notables, while the English team was captained by Flight Sergeant Cyril Washbrook, and since I had always been an avid follower of county cricket, a host of names I had known for years. Many years later I was visiting the Australian Houses of Parliament at Canberra; our guide was very obviously a cricket enthusiast, so I recounted this story to him; he was able to recite the names of all eleven of the Australian players who took part! The party was still in full swing when I left to catch my midnight train to South Wales; it was a memorable evening indeed. My only regret is that I did not get them all to autograph a copy of the menu. It would be a unique document.

Another memorable evening was a few nights later when we assembled in the Officers' Mess to listen to Churchill's speech announcing the end of hostilities. The other memory I took away from Talbenny is the sight of thousands of sea-birds fluttering up from Skomer as we took off - the flight path from the main runway passing directly over the islet, now a Nature Reserve.

While at Talbenny - we were there for two and a half months - our only ferry delivery was to take an Anson to Algiers; it was going to a minor Arab royal in the Middle East and was most luxuriously equipped. That, however, even with pre-delivery testing and the return flight took only about ten days, so we were pretty bored most of the time, and I wasn't sorry when my pilot, who was something of a socialite and seemed to have connections at the Air Ministry, was able to persuade someone there to send us on a course to convert to Dakotas - DC-3s - with a view to joining one of the Dakota squadrons operating much more regularly. His connection proved to be a very useful one, as we were soon posted to another Transport Command OTU, this one No.109 at Wymeswold near Loughborough, where we spent a fortnight converting to Dakotas before joining 147 Squadron at Croydon. Our lives were transformed, for not only were we near London, but we had a real job to do. 147 Squadron was carrying passengers every day to all the big cities of northwestern Europe;

we would fly to Paris one day, Berlin the next, Brussels, Hamburg, Copenhagen, Oslo, and so on, and the schedules were so arranged that we would night-stop from time to time, especially at the more attractive destinations such as Copenhagen.

Copenhagen was also worth visiting for another reason; while we weren't exactly starving in England, there were many items still severely rationed, and many shortages; Denmark, on the other hand, was well looked after by the Germans as part of their 'larder', but suffered from an almost complete lack of cigarettes. We bartered! The standard rate was 100 cigarettes for 30 dozen eggs; we could also obtain much other farm produce - ham, bacon, cheese, meat. On one occasion I acquired a whole Danish Blue cheese, which had such a pungent odour that the other two members of the crew insisted that it be removed from the flight deck and placed in the passenger compartment! Many Danish shops were far better stocked than those in England, and I was able to buy our first dinner and tea set from a large store in Copenhagen.

The flight to Oslo was also an interesting one, for it was emphasised at briefing how essential it was to fly up the right fiord; if one chose the wrong one, the fiord was too narrow to turn round to make an exit, and the Dakota lacked the power to climb steeply out over the mountains! I was very careful to select the right fiord!

From time to time we carried interesting passengers; one was the well-known Daily Express war correspondent, Alan Moorehead, though he did sleep most of the journey; another was Ivy Benson, leader of the all-ladies dance-band whom we took to Brussels where she was arranging a concert for her band. Another interesting experience was our first landing using GCA, Ground Controlled Approach. We were on a flight to Hamburg, and conditions got worse and worse from the Dutch coast onwards. When we arrived, I thought, "We shall never be able to land here," but a very confident voice started talking us down, giving us very, very detailed instructions, to which, of course, I was able to listen just as well as the pilot could.

TRANSPORT COMMAND

The final instruction was, "When you see the runway, go ahead and land." At that very moment we saw the runway appearing out of the murk in front of us. Conditions were so bad, even on the ground, that we had to follow a van sent out to guide us in, and when we did stop just by the control tower, I noticed that the RAF Ensign flying above it was actually in cloud; conditions couldn't have been much worse; it was a very impressive experience indeed, and gave us great confidence in GCA for the future.

Chapter 15

BOAC (British Overseas Airways Corporation)
December 1945–January 1947

We were at Croydon from September till December, then just after Christmas BOAC announced that it required more navigators, so I thought the time had come to use my Civil Air Navigator's Licence. Strictly, this is post-war experience, of course, as was the spell at Croydon, for I had listened to Churchill's speech announcing the end of the war at Talbenny. However, it seems all part of my war-time experience, for I should not have had the opportunity if I had not been a navigator in the RAF. In early January, I was posted from Croydon to Whitchurch, just outside Bristol, where all aircrew transferring from the RAF to BOAC - and there were considerable numbers at this time, of course - were sent to undertake a course to familiarise themselves with civilian methods. It was a thorough training lasting about two months at what was known as CTS - Civil Training School. Most of the work was in the classroom, but we flew one or two cross-country navigation exercises, and all had to undertake two flights outside the war zone of Europe, which didn't leave much scope, of course. I did one flight to Stockholm and one to Lisbon; we carried two navigators, one of whom navigated on the outward flight, and the other on the homeward, meanwhile the one not actually navigating practised astro in the astro-dome. We had to fly first to Hurn, now Bournemouth International Airport, to clear Customs, there being no Customs at Whitchurch. In spite of currency restrictions on the amount of sterling we were allowed, we returned laden with goods we hadn't been able to obtain for a long time, especially from Portugal, when we were able to purchase fruit we hadn't seen for years.

At the end of the course we were posted to various BOAC lines - the equivalent of an RAF Squadron. Most of us, I think, hoped for a posting to London Airport for the Transatlantic route, but I was quite happy to join No. 4 Line which operated flying-boats out of Poole Harbour to Singapore, and whose maintenance base and administrative headquarters was at Hythe, on Southampton Water, only 15 minutes on the ferry from Southampton.

The BOAC flying-boats, themselves known as Hythes, were, in fact, ex-RAF Sunderlands with the gun-turrets fared in and the interior comfortably furnished for passengers. They were quite elephantine in size, internally scarcely smaller than a modern 'jumbo' yet we carried only 25 passengers. It was all very comfortable; it was also very leisurely, for the Hythes cruised only at about 130 knots, had a range of only about 800 miles, so that we had to make frequent landings to refuel, and were not pressurised, so that we rarely flew higher than 6,000 to 8,000 feet.

I was sent down the route once with a BOAC experienced navigator; we flew to Singapore and back, which normally took crews 18 days, and then I was on my own. There was no regular crew as I had always been used to in the RAF, both in Bomber and Transport Commands. One turned up to find that one was scheduled to fly with a certain Captain, a certain First Officer, a certain Radio Officer and a certain Flight Engineer, and off we went; in the year I spent with BOAC I never flew more than once with the same aircrew member of any category. There were also seven or eight stewards under a Senior Steward who was usually an ex-Merchant Navy seaman.

Navigation was, by RAF standards, fairly primitive. I had a great deal of respect for these old pre-war Imperial Airways pilots, but they knew very little about radar, and didn't really want to know anything about it; they had always managed perfectly well without radar, and as far as they were concerned, they would go on managing without it! The navigator had an air-speed indicator, an altimeter, a driftmeter, a sextant, and an astrocompass, and occasionally the assistance of a radio bearing, but much of the navigation was simply by pinpointing places one passed over and by taking visual bearings to obtain position lines, which was fine in good weather conditions, but less satisfactory when the weather deteriorated.

The Navigating Officer had other duties, too. In those days there was no radio-telephone contact between the flight-deck and the passenger cabin, so it was up to him to keep the passengers supplied with information; at least once an hour he had to provide an information sheet for the passengers telling them where they were, what they could expect to see on either side of the aircraft in the next hour, the height and speed over the ground, and the ETA at the next destination. Another duty was to climb on top of the aircraft through the astrodome if the pilot had to turn in choppy water; he would then walk to the wing-tip to keep the float on that side down in the water so that the pilot could execute his turn; I didn't have to do this on many occasions, but it was an interesting new task! Yet another was to sit halfway out of the astrodome when engines were being started up holding the fire extinguisher, so that if one of the engines caught fire as it was being started, the navigator could dash along the wing to dowse the fire; I've always been glad that I was never called upon to perform this particular part of a Navigating Officer's duty!

Our passengers were assembled at Airways Terminal in London and travelled by train to Poole, where they were accommodated at the Harbour Heights Hotel. The crew, too, arrived at the same hotel during the afternoon, and after a leisurely meal together, retired early since we always left at first light the next morning. The flying boats looked very elegant if one was watching them take off, but inside the boat it sounded, as someone once said, 'like dragging a rake across a corrugated tin roof.' Fortunately, my experience at Pensacola had prepared me for the din. The first leg of our journey took us from Poole to Marseilles, a flight of between four and a half and five hours. We never normally night-stopped there, but flew on another five hours to Augusta in Sicily, previously an Italian naval flying-boat base. The schedule was so arranged that although the passengers went on the following morning with a crew already there, the crew spent two nights at Augusta, a most attractive place to stay with water-skiing and swimming off the jetty in almost guaranteed sunshine. Our blue uniforms were left there to be cleaned and pressed while we were further east, and we changed into khaki drill, picking up our blue uniform on our return journey. After two delightful days at Augusta, we flew on to Cairo, a six and a half hour flight. Landing on the Nile provided quite a tricky task for the Engineer, as it was his responsibility to slip a boat hook through a loop of rope on one of the buoys. Since the Nile is quite a fast-flowing river, this was not easy, but woe betide him if he missed first time, as he occasionally did, for the Captains were never happy to have to go round again. They regarded it as a slight on their professional reputation if they didn't moor up first time.

From Cairo, usually after a night-stop on a house-boat on the Nile, to Basra was a further six hours. Once you had crossed the Suez Canal, there was little to see except desert, apart from the Dead Sea. Flights then had to keep north of Saudi Arabia as the King, Abdul Aziz Ibn Saud, did not allow flights across his kingdom. However, if you flew too far north, you could probably see the pipeline across the desert, and eventually you would see the Euphrates and land close to its confluence with the Tigris. On one occasion we were flying quietly across the desert in a cloudless sky, when we suddenly hit a ferocious up-current of air; all my navigation equipment flew into the air off my chart-table and deposited itself all round the flight deck; one or two of the passengers sustained minor cuts and bruises, but it was all over in a moment; one of the dangers of not being able to fly high enough to get over the turbulence.

Another two and a quarter hours flying took us down the Red Sea to Bahrain, and then between six and six and a half hours almost due east to Karachi. We crossed Qatar, and then the Oman Peninsula, certainly the most desolate landscape I had ever seen. Baluchistan was on our port beam as we flew on to Karachi, where crews broke their journey again. We nearly all used to visit a cobbler there; we carried a cut-out of the feet of our wife or fiancée, and he would make a very nice pair of sandals which could be collected on the way home.

Clothes and shoes were still rationed in the UK, so they were very acceptable; they cost twelve rupees, about eighteen shillings.

An incident occurred at Karachi which I recall with amusement. When we stayed at hotels down the route, the Captain normally stayed at one hotel, the professional aircrew at another, and the stewards at yet a third - there were no stewardesses in those days, of course. On one occasion at Karachi, by some mischance, the Chief Steward was accommodated in the same hotel as the aircrew; I don't think it worried the aircrew in the least, but the Captain was horrified, and felt it necessary to see each member of the crew personally to apologise for the indignity we had suffered in having a steward in our hotel! It was a different world, of course.

We carried as far as Karachi on one occasion a group of six French models, mannequins as we called them then. They embarked at Marseilles and were going to Australia as France attempted to rebuild its export market. As we travelled further east and south, the climate became hotter and hotter, for there was no air conditioning on aircraft then, and these six exceedingly glamorous young ladies started to divest themselves of their garments till by the time we were nearing Karachi, one would not have thought they could remove a further item and remain respectable. I never knew the flight crew so solicitous for the welfare of passengers; so many visits were made to the passenger cabin that it seemed at times there was hardly anyone remaining on the flight deck!

The next leg, across India, was quite the longest stretch of the journey, taking between eight and eight and a half hours, so we were just about at the limit of our range. Fortunately, there was a lake between Karachi and Calcutta for use in emergency, and once on the homeward route, flying into a headwind and petrol getting low, we took the precaution of landing there. Calcutta was, I found, unbearably hot; in temperature it probably was not quite as hot as Bahrain, but Bahrain's heat was dry, whereas at Calcutta the humidity was so high that I was always glad to get back into the air a few thousand feet to cool down. I never once night-stopped there, which was probably a blessing, although in other ways I regret this is one of the world's great cities that I have never seen.

A four-hour flight took us from the River Hooghly, just north of the Willingdon Bridge, where we had landed, to Rangoon in the great wide estuary of the River Rangoon, which is really, I suppose, part of the Delta of the Irrawaddy. It was quite a distance in a launch from the landing site back to the jetty; on one occasion, I had hardly put my foot on the bottom step of the jetty when a voice above me exclaimed "Arthur!" It was my old friend George Brantingham - now Squadron Leader Brantingham, DFC and Bar, Command Navigation Officer - who was there to welcome one of our passengers (years later he told me he had been meeting one of Mountbatten's daughters); after leaving 97, he had served as a navigation instructor for a while at an OTU, then crewed up with a pilot who was going to the Far East to fly Liberators on very long-range bombing operations against the Japanese in Malaya. After the completion of his second tour, he had returned to the UK to undertake the Spec. N (Special Navigation) course at Shawbury, so was very well qualified for his senior role.

A further flight of about five and a half hours took us to Penang, not normally a night-stop, but where we sat on the shore under sunshades while the Hythe was being refuelled, drinking fresh cold fruit juice and eating mangosteen. The final leg to Singapore took another three hours, a total for the journey from Poole of between fifty-five and sixty hours flying spread over nine days, nearly all of it in daylight. The passengers would reach Sydney four or five days after leaving Poole; a QANTAS crew would be waiting for them in Singapore, and would take them on to Jakarta, Darwin, and so to Sydney.

While on the route I managed to renew acquaintance with several of my sixth-form classmates. In Karachi I met Crosby Hunter; in Rangoon I met up again with Sergeant Bill Blight, the friend with whom I had been billeted in Bournemouth during the first year of the war; in Singapore I saw Capt Peter Vincent, seconded from the army to the Singapore Police Force, and Flight Lieutenant 'Cuthbert' Emmet, a radar officer. I also met Commander 'Cleeve' Clowser, Head of Geography at Taunton's School, but now serving at the naval headquarters on the island.

We always had a break of two days at Singapore before setting out on the return journey, the same route in reverse. One remembered to pick up sandals at Karachi; silk stockings and wine, marsala, at Augusta, and also change back into blue there; taking off from Augusta, some of the Captains would always make a point of circling Mount Etna with its wisp of smoke blowing from the crater before setting off on the final leg back to Poole eighteen days after setting out. There was supposed to be a guarantee of seven days at home after each service flight, not all leave, because crews had to go to Hythe for debriefing one day, but on one occasion I had been at home only three days when I received a telegram requiring me to be at Poole for the next day's service.

Two of our flights took a slightly different route. From Rangoon, we flew to Bangkok, a flight of six hours, then on across the River Mekong to Hong Kong; the route was fairly close to Hanoi, but we were briefed to stay clear of the city because there was already trouble in what was then French Indo-China and anti-aircraft fire had frequently been seen above Hanoi. We flew on across the South China Sea, traversing Hainan, intensively cultivated, to arrive in Hong Kong six and a half hours after leaving Bangkok. Landing there then was very different from today; there wasn't a single skyscraper to be seen; our first flight to Hong Kong made a small piece of aviation history, as on August 27th 1946, we were the first civil aircraft to land in Hong Kong after the war.

I flew with BOAC for just over a year, the final eight months of my RAF service on secondment, then six months on contract as a civilian. The Corporation offered me a post as an instructor at their School, which had now moved to Aldermaston, but even then I could see very little future for navigators in civil aviation, and events soon proved me right. Time was running out for the flying boats, too. They were slow and uneconomic. Moreover, BOAC was the only airline operating boats, which meant that they alone were responsible for maintaining the bases from which they operated with the expense of launches and ground staff who could not be shared with other lines. In fact, BOAC continued to operate them for only another two years; they went out of service in November 1950.

Conclusion

My flying days were almost over; but not quite, for the post-war RAFVR (Volunteer Reserve) opened up in the summer of 1948, and since there was a base, Hamble, only 5 miles away from the village where we had set up home in Hampshire, I joined, and enjoyed about forty hours flying a year, mainly at weekends, but with a fortnight's annual training every summer. Flying was mainly navigational exercises in Ansons, but there was an occasional flight into Europe, and I had the opportunity to fly on the Berlin Airlift for a few weeks, at about the time that the operation was coming to an end. I note from my log-book that the load we most commonly carried - in Dakotas once more - was coal. Flying continued at Hamble, No. 14 Reserve School, till the summer of 1953, when the incoming administration, desirous of making cuts in government spending, closed most of the Reserve Schools. However, No. 15, at Redhill, survived another year, and I did a fortnight's summer training there in 1954. Then the remaining Reserve Schools were closed, and although I held a war appointment post at HQ Transport Command for about five more years, that really was the end of my days in aviation, and therefore a suitable place to end this story.

A few years after the war, a memorial was built at Runnymede for those airmen with no known grave. It was unveiled by the Queen in

1953. My parents, my wife and I were asked to represent the Munro family, Jimmy's parents and two brothers; we did so gladly, but with great sadness.

My wife and I also represented Jimmy's brothers at the unveiling of the Canada Memorial in Green Park on 3rd June 1994.

As I write these notes, I anticipate - D.V. - being present at the unveiling of the Bomber Command Memorial in Green Park in 2011.

A.H.G.S.
September 2010.

Addendum

Much to my surprise, I find myself (more than ten years since the last!) adding - at the request of Granddaughter, Amy, who was responsible for the hard copy of this memoir - a further addendum!

In June 2012, a year later than I had anticipated, my wife and I, accompanied by our two daughters, attended the long-awaited unveiling of the Bomber Command Memorial in Green Park.

Three years later, in October 2015, Eva and I travelled to Lincoln for the "unveiling" of the 102-feet high spire at the International Bomber Command Centre, a department of Lincoln University. A whole day's programme of events was hosted by the historian, Dan Snow.

Forward to June 2017, and we were once more in Green Park to celebrate the 5th anniversary of the monument's unveiling. After a short service, I found myself in conversation with the Israeli Ambassador, who told me he had great admiration for Bomber Command since his father had escaped from his Nazi captors during an attack on Magdeburg. We then adjourned to the RAF Club, almost opposite the Memorial, for a buffet lunch; Sir Stephen Hillier, the Chief of the Air Staff, drew my attention to a painting in the Gallery of a Lancaster over Peenemünde on 17 August, 1943.

The following year, there was a further ceremony at Lincoln to open fully the Centre now that a Memorial Wall, listing every one of Bomber Command's 55,573 casualties in World War 2, had been built around the Spire. I was able to take a photograph of that section of the wall showing the name of my 19 year-old Canadian pilot, Jimmy, and send it to his family in Ontario.

Finally, Eva and I visited Lincolnshire once more in September 2021 to attend the last Reunion of 97 Squadron Association - the last because the Association has now disbanded itself! The Reunion commenced with a short service in the Station Chapel at RAF Coningsby. The small building is aglow with colour from the seven stained-glass windows, each of which is dedicated to a squadron which flew from Coningsby or its satellite, Woodhall. I was astounded to see that the Lancaster featured in the 97 Squadron window was OF-J, the very aircraft in which we had flown the great majority of our two tours of operations!

Epilogue
Two different points of view

St Crispian's Eve – King Henry V

This day is called the feast of Crispian.
He that outlives this day, and comes safe home,
Will stand a tip-toe when the day is named,
And rouse him at the name of Crispian.
He that shall live this day, and see old age,
Will yearly on the vigil feast his neighbours,
And say 'To-morrow is Saint Crispian'.
Then will he strip his sleeve and show his scars.
And say 'These wounds I had on Crispian's day.'
Old men forget: yet all shall be forgot,
But he'll remember with advantages,
What feats he did that day. Then shall our names,
Familiar in his mouth as household words –
Harry the King, Bedford and Exeter,
Warwick and Talbot, Salisbury and Gloucester,
Be in their flowing cups freshly remember'd.
This story shall the good man teach his son;
And Crispin Crispian shall ne'er go by,
From this day to the ending of the world,
But we in it shall be remember'd;
We few, we happy few, we band of brothers;

For he to-day that sheds his blood with me
Shall be my brother; be he ne'er so vile,
This day shall gentle his condition.
And gentlemen in England now a-bed
Shall think themselves accursed they were not here,
And hold their manhoods cheap whiles any speaks
That fought with us upon Saint Crispin's day.

From King Henry V, Act IV, Scene III
(William Shakespeare)

Epilogue to 'Death of a Hero', by Richard Aldington

Eleven years after the fall of Troy,
We, the old men - some of us nearly forty -
Met and talked on the sunny rampart
Over our wine, while the lizards scuttled
In dusty grass, and the crickets chirred.

Some bared their wounds;
Some spoke of the thirst, dry in the throat,
And the heart-beat in the din of battle;
Some spoke of intolerable sufferings,
The brightness gone from their eyes
And the grey already thick in their hair.

And I sat a little apart
From the garrulous talk and old memories,
And I heard a boy of twenty
Say petulantly to a girl, seizing her arm:
"Oh, come away; why do you stand there
Listening open-mouthed to the talk of old men?

EPILOGUE

Haven't you heard enough of Troy and Achilles?
Why should they bore us for ever
With an old quarrel and the names of dead men
We never knew, and dull forgotten battles?"

And he drew her away,
And she looked back and laughed
As he spoke more contempt of us,
Being now out of hearing.

And I thought of the graves by desolate Troy
And the beauty of many young men now in dust,
And the long agony, and how useless it all was.
And the talk still clashed about me
Like the meeting of blade and blade.

And as they two moved away
He put an arm about her, and kissed her;
And afterwards I heard their gay distant laughter.
And I looked at the hollow cheeks
And the weary eyes and the grey-streaked heads
Of the old men - nearly forty - about me;
And I too walked away
In an agony of helpless grief and pity.

Richard Aldington's poem 'Epilogue to Death of a Hero' (c) the Estate of Richard Aldington, all rights reserved, included by kind permission of the Estate c/o Rosica Colin Limited, London

Bibliography

Bending, Kevin ACHIEVE YOUR AIM - THE HISTORY OF 97 (Straits settlement) SQUADRON
Woodfield Publishing 2005

Chorley, W.R. BOMBER COMMAND LOSSES 1943
Midland Counties Publications 1996

Middlebrook, Martin and Everitt, Chris THE BOMBER COMMAND WAR DIARIES
Viking 1985

Middlebrook, Martin The PEENEMUNDE RAID
Penguin 1982

Middlebrook, Martin The BATTLE OF HAMBURG
Penguin 1984

Middlebrook, Martin The BERLIN RAIDS
Penguin 1988

Richards, Denis The HARDEST VICTORY
Hodder & Stoughton 1994

Terraine, John The RIGHT OF THE LINE
Hodder & Stoughton 1985